2 -

11/
19

One Prayer at a Time

....

One Prayer at a Time

A TWELVE-STEP ANTHOLOGY FOR PEOPLE IN RECOVERY AND ALL WHO SEEK A DEEPER FAITH

EDITED BY

F. Forrester Church and Terrence J. Mulry

COLLIER BOOKS
MACMILLAN PUBLISHING COMPANY
New York

COLLIER MACMILLAN PUBLISHERS
London

Collier Books
Macmillan Publishing Company
866 Third Avenue, New York, NY 10022
Collier Macmillan Canada, Inc.

Library of Congress Cataloging-in-Publication Data
One prayer at a time: a 12 step anthology for people in
recovery and all who seek a deeper faith/edited by F.
Forrester Church and Terrence J. Mulry.
　　p. cm.
　　ISBN 0-02-031070-6
　　　1. Alcoholics—Prayer-books and devotions—English.
2. Narcotic addicts—Prayer-books and devotions—English.
3. Gamblers—Prayer-books and devotions—English.
I. Church, F. Forrester.　　II. Mulry, Terrence J.
BL625.45.054　　1989
291.4'3—dc20　　89-7072　　CIP

Macmillan books are available at special discounts for bulk
purchases for sales promotions, premiums, fund-raising, or
educational use. For details, contact:

Special Sales Director
Macmillan Publishing Company
866 Third Avenue
New York, NY 10022

10 9 8 7 6 5 4 3 2 1

Printed in the United States of America

Contents

....

Preface

Millions of people who have suffered from addictive illnesses have begun to recover and continue to recover in twelve-step programs. The secret to the extraordinary success of these programs is that they are informed by a simple but profound set of spiritual principles. These principles are in no way sectarian; in fact, they resonate with teachings of all of the world's great religions. People who have lost control over their lives, who have bottomed out or fallen into the abyss, are saved from the devastation of their addiction (itself a kind of God substitute) by acknowledging their powerlessness, reaching out to a power greater than themselves for help, taking a fearless moral inventory, confessing the wrongs they have done to themselves and others, acting to change their behavior and to make amends for past injuries, and then seeking to build a closer relationship with God (as they understand God) and their neighbors. They do this one day at a time. Without taking on a self-righteous, sanctimonious air of "the reformed," people who once were in thrall to alcohol, drugs, gambling, or eating disorders, and who follow these steps toward recovery, develop and then continue to cultivate a rich spirituality, one that sustains them through good times and bad.

We have compiled this anthology of prayers from many traditions both as an aid to people in recovery from addiction and also as a devotional guide for anyone who wishes to deepen his or her spiritual life. It's a simple idea, really. We have taken the major theme of the twelve steps and selected twelve prayers for each. For instance, if you wish to reflect and pray on the theme of powerlessness, you will find twelve prayers on it in the first chapter, and so on throughout the twelve steps.

Each of the chapters begins with a psalm, those ancient Hebrew hymns that explore our relationship with God in all its aspects: loving, fearful, angry, close, distant. Beyond this, we have deliberately cast a broad net. We include prayers from Christians (Protestant, Greek Orthodox and Roman Catholic), Jews, Muslims, Buddhists, Hindus, and a number of philosophical schools. Our selections come from Africa, Asia, Europe, and America. Some are drawn from the world's scriptures, others from great religious leaders, and still others from anonymous authors. Several are written by women. Some will be more familiar to you than others, but each is chosen for its spiritual depth and its appropriateness to one of the twelve steps.

The first chapter, "Out of the Depths," covers the themes of admission and powerlessness. The second and third chapters, "I Cried unto Thee" and "The Lord Is My Shepherd," invite us to reach out to God for help. Chapters four through seven encourage us to examine ourselves honestly and fearlessly; to confess our sins; and to seek God's assistance in changing our lives by helping us to remove our shortcomings. These chapters are entitled "Why Boast in Mischief?", "Have Mercy on Me," "I Will Extol Thee," and

"I Will Lift Up Mine Eyes." Chapters eight and nine, "Even the Sparrow Finds a Home" and "How Good and Pleasant It Is," deal with restoring healthy relationships with others. The tenth chapter, "This Is the Day," continues the exploration of our relationship with God, ourselves, and others by focusing attention on a single day in our lives. Chapters eleven and twelve, "Thou Preservest Me from Trouble" and "Let the Redeemed of the Lord Say So," further encourage us to deepen our relationship with God through meditation and prayer, and then to carry our message to others while practicing the spiritual principles that restore and sustain health.

As a devotional guide, this anthology can be used in many ways. For some it will be the beginning of a life of prayer. For others it will serve as a resource to help deepen an already active spiritual life. The wonderful thing about prayer—and the twelve steps in general—is that we may begin wherever we are and receive immediate help and sustenance.

We wish to thank the following individuals and publishing houses for permission to reprint those prayers not in the public domain: *Adventures in Prayer* by Charles Henry Brent (New York: Harper & Row, 1940); *Alive to God* compiled by Kenneth Cragg (London: Oxford University Press, 1970); *A Book of Public Prayer* by Harry Emerson Fosdick (New York: Harper & Row, 1964); *Devotional Services for Public Worship* by John Hunter (London: J. M. Dent, 1964); *A Diary of Private Prayer* by John Baillie (London: Oxford University Press, 1949); *The Flower Ornament Scripture* translated by Thomas Cleary (Boston: Shambhala, 1987); *The Holy Bible*, Revised Standard Version copyright 1946, © 1952, 1971 by the Director of Christian Education of the National Council of Churches of Christ in the U.S.A.; *I Lie on My Mat and Pray* edited by Fritz Pawelzik (New York: Friendship Press, 1964); *Life in the Spirit* edited by Kathryn

Spink (New York: Harper & Row, 1985); *Markings* by Dag Hammarskjöld, translated by Leif Sjoberg and W. H. Auden, copyright © 1964 by Alfred A. Knopf, Inc., and Faber & Faber Ltd., reprinted by permission of Alfred A. Knopf, Inc.; *New Seeds of Contemplation* by Thomas Merton, copyright © 1961 by The Abbey of Gethsemani, Inc., reprinted by permission of New Directions Publishing Corporation; *Prayers for Dark People* by W. E. B. Du Bois, edited by Herbert Aptheker (Amherst: University of Massachusetts Press, 1980); *Prayers for Help and Healing* edited by William Barclay (New York: Harper & Row, 1980); *Poems of Henry Van Dyke* by Henry Van Dyke (New York: Charles Scribner & Sons, 1940); *The Wisdom of India and China* edited by Lin Yutang, copyright 1942, © 1970 by Random House, Inc., reprinted by permission of Random House, Inc.; *The World at One in Prayer* edited by Daniel J. Fleming (New York: Harper & Brothers, 1942). If any citation in the foregoing is inaccurate or if any copyrighted material was inadvertently included in the text, corrections will be made in future editions.

Compiling these prayers has again revealed to us the miracle of the transforming process itself, from the prayers of helplessness in the first chapter through the prayers of thanksgiving in the twelfth. Whether you think of the twelve steps as a ladder or as a spiral, and however you define the "higher power" to whom you pray, it is our sincere hope that these prayers will be of assistance to you in your search for spiritual growth and wholeness—one prayer at a time.

F. Forrester Church

Terrence J. Mulry

One Prayer at a Time

....

1

....

Out of the Depths

Self-recognition, or admission of one's fundamental condition, is the basis for all true humility, all true spirituality, all true growth. In a paradoxical way, what initially seems like the most painful reality—a condition of hopelessness and helplessness—in fact helps us to come to terms with the human condition itself. We cannot go on alone, fearful and self-demanding. But we need not go on alone. Indeed, it is better to go on with others.

The Zen master claps and the novice recognizes reality. The Prodigal ceases to gain from a life of riotous living and returns asking to be a servant, and he is joyously welcomed home. Life begins anew.

In the first three steps, we forge a relationship with the reality of God's grace in our lives. This relationship steels us for the journey ahead.

Out of the depths have I cried unto thee, O Lord. Lord, hear my voice: let thine ears be attentive to the voice of my supplications. If thou, Lord, shouldest mark iniquities, O Lord, who shall stand? But there is forgiveness with thee, that thou mayest be feared. I wait for the Lord, my soul doth wait, and in his word do I hope. My soul waiteth for the Lord more than they that watch for the morning: I say, more than they that watch for the morning. Let Israel hope in the Lord: for with the Lord there is mercy, and with him is plenteous redemption. And he shall redeem Israel from all his iniquities.

PSALM 130

O Lord my God, the amazing horrors of darkness were gathered around me and covered me all over, and I saw no way to go forth: I felt the depth and extent of the misery of my fellow creatures separated from the divine harmony, and it was heavier than I could bear, and I was crushed down under it. I lifted up my hand, I stretched out my arm, but there was none to help me; I looked round about and was amazed; in the depths of misery, O Lord, I remembered that thou art omnipotent, that I had called thee Father, and I felt that I loved thee, and I was made quiet in thy will, and I waited for deliverance from thee; thou hadst pity upon me when no man could help me. I saw that meekness under suffering was showed to us in the most affecting example of thy Son, and thou taught me to follow him, and I said, "Thy will, O Father, be done."

JOHN WOOLMAN

I have no other helper than you,
no other father,
no other redeemer,
no other support.
I pray to you.
Only you can help me.
My present misery
is too great.
Despair grips me,
and I am at my wits' end.
I am sunk in the depths,
and I cannot pull myself up
or out.
If it is your will,
help me out of this misery.
Let me know
that you are stronger
than all misery and all enemies.
O Lord, if I come through this,
please let the experience
contribute to my and my brothers' blessing.
You will not forsake me;
this I know.
Amen.

AFRICAN PRAYER

4

Lo, I am of small account.
What shall I answer thee? . . .
I have uttered that which I did not understand,
Things too wonderful for me, which I did not
    know. . . .
I knew thee only by hearsay,
But now my eye has seen thee.
Therefore I retract and repent,
In dust and ashes.

BOOK OF JOB

O God, teach us to know that failure is as much a part
of life as success—and whether it shall be evil or good
depends upon the way we meet it; if we face it listlessly
and daunted, angrily or vengefully, then indeed is it evil
for it spells death. But if we let our failures stand as
guideposts and as warnings—as beacons and as
guardians—then is honest failure far better than stolen
success, and but a part of that great training which God
gives us to make us women and men. The race is not to
the swift—nor the battle to the strong, O God.

W. E. B. DuBois

I fled thee, down the nights and down the days;
I fled thee, down the arches of the years;
I fled thee, down the labyrinthine ways
Of my own mind; and in the mist of tears
I hid from thee, and under running laughter.

5

Up vistaed hopes I sped;
And shot, precipitated,
Adown Titanic glooms of chasmed fears,
From those strong Feet that followed, followed
   after.
But with unhurrying chase,
And unperturbed pace,
Deliberate speed, majestic instancy,
They beat—and a Voice beat
More instant than the Feet—
"All things betray thee, who betrayest me."
I pleaded, outlaw-wise,
By many a hearted casement, curtained red,
Trellised with intertwining charities;
(For, though I knew thy love who followed,
Yet was I sore adread
Lest, having thee, I must have naught beside.)
But, if one little casement parted wide,
The gust of thy approach would clash it to:
Fear wist not to evade, as Love wist to pursue.
Across the margent of the world I fled,
And troubled the gold gateways of the stars,
Smiting for shelter on their clanged bars;
Fretted to dulcet jars
And silvern chatter the pale ports o' the moon.
I said to Dawn: "Be sudden"—to Eve: "Be soon;
With thy young skiey blossoms heap me over
From this tremendous Lover—
Float thy vague veil about me, lest he see!"
I tempted all thy servitors, but to find
My own betrayal in their constancy,
In faith to thee their fickleness to me,
Their traitorous trueness, and their loyal deceit.
To all swift things for swiftness did I sue;
Clung to the whistling mane of every wind.

But whether they swept, smoothly fleet,
The long savannahs of the blue;
Or whether, Thunder-driven,
They clanged his chariot 'thwart a heaven,
Plashy with flying lightnings round the spurn o'
  their feet:—
Fear wist not to evade as Love wist to pursue.
Still with unhurrying chase,
And unperturbed pace,
Deliberate speed, majestic instancy,
Came on the following Feet,
And a Voice above their beat—
"Naught shelters thee, who wilt not shelter me."
I sought no more that after which I strayed
In face of man or maid;
But still within the little children's eyes
Seems something, something that replies,
They at least are for me, surely for me!
I turned me to them very wistfully;
But just as their young eyes grew sudden fair
With dawning answers there,
Their angel plucked them from me by the hair.
"Come then, ye other children, Nature's—share
With me" (said I) "your delicate fellowship;
Let me greet you lip to lip,
Let me twine with you caresses,
Wantoning
With our Lady-Mother's vagrant tresses,
Banqueting
With her in her wind-walled palace,
Underneath her azured dais,
Quaffing, as your taintless way is,
From a chalice
Lucent-weeping out of the dayspring."
So it was done:

7

I in their delicate fellowship was one—
Drew the bolt of Nature's secrecies.
I knew all the swift importings
On the willful face of skies;
I knew how the clouds arise
Spumed of the wild sea-snortings;
All that's born or dies
Rose and drooped with; made them shapers
Of mine own moods, or wailful or divine;
With them joyed and was bereaven.
I was heavy with the even,
When she lit her glimmering tapers
Round the day's dead sanctities.
I laughed in the morning's eyes.
I triumphed and I saddened with all weather,
Heaven and I wept together,
And its sweet tears were salt with mortal mine;
Against the red throb of its sunset-heart
I laid my own to beat,
And share commingling heat;
But not by that, by that, was eased my human
    smart.
In vain my tears were wet on Heaven's gray cheek.
For ah! we know not what each other says,
These things and I; in sound I speak—
Their sound is but their stir, they speak by silences.
Nature, poor stepdame, cannot slake my drouth;
Let her, if she would owe me,
Drop yon blue bosom-veil of sky, and show me
The breasts o' her tenderness:
Never did any milk of hers once bless
My thirsting mouth.
Nigh and nigh draws the chase,
With unperturbed pace,
Deliberate speed, majestic instancy;

And past those noised Feet
A voice comes yet more fleet—
"Lo! naught contents thee, who content'st
  not me."
Naked I wait thy love's uplifted stroke!
My harness piece by piece thou hast hewn from me,
And smitten me to my knee;
I am defenseless utterly.
I slept, methinks, and woke,
And, slowly gazing, find me stripped in sleep.
In the rash lustihead of my young powers,
I shook the pillaring hours
And pulled my life upon me; grimed with smears,
I stand amid the dust o' the mounded years—
My mangled youth lies dead beneath the heap.
My days have crackled and gone up in smoke,
Have puffed and burst as sun-starts on a stream.
Yea, faileth now even dream
The dreamer, and the lute the lutanist;
Even the linked fantasies, in whose blossomy twist
I swung the earth a trinket at my wrist,
Are yielding; cords of all too weak account
For earth with heavy griefs so overplussed.
Ah! is thy love indeed
A weed, albeit an amaranthine weed,
Suffering no flowers except its own to mount?
Ah! must—
Designer infinite!—
Ah! must thou char the wood ere thou canst limn
with it?
My freshness spent its wavering shower i' the dust;
And now my heart is as a broken fount,
Wherein tear-drippings stagnate, spilt down ever
From the dank thoughts that shiver
Upon the sighful branches of my mind.

Such is; what is to be?
The pulp so bitter, how shall taste the rind?
I dimly guess what Time in mists confounds;
Yet ever and anon a trumpet sounds
From the hid battlements of Eternity;
Those shaken mists a space unsettle, then
Round the half-glimpsed turrets slowly wash again.
But not ere him who summoneth
I first have seen, enwound
With glooming robes purpureal, cypress-crowned;
Thy name I know, and what his trumpet saith.
Whether man's heart or life it be which yields
Thee harvest, must thy harvest-fields
Be dunged with rotten death?
Now of that long pursuit
Comes on at hand the bruit;
Thy Voice is round me like a bursting sea:
"And is thy earth so marred,
Shattered in shard on shard?
Lo, all things fly thee, for thou fliest me!
Strange, piteous, futile thing!
Wherefore should any set thy love apart?
Seeing none but I makes much of naught" (thou
      said),
"And human love needs human meriting:
How hast thou merited—
Of all man's clotted clay the dingiest clot?
Alack, thou knowest not
How little worthy of any love thou art!
Whom wilt thou find to love ignoble thee,
Save me, save only me?
All which I took from thee I did but take,
Not for thy harms,
But just that thou might'st seek it in my arms.

All which thy child's mistake
Fancies as lost, I have stored for thee at home:
Rise, clasp my hand, and come!"

Halts by me that footfall:
Is my gloom, after all,
Shade of thy hand, outstretched caressingly?
"Ah, fondest, blindest, weakest,
I am he whom thou seekest!
Thou dravest love from thee, who dravest me."
ADAPTED FROM FRANCIS THOMPSON,
"THE HOUND OF HEAVEN"

Blessed be thy name, O Lord, forever, who hast
permitted this tribulation to come upon me! I am not
able to fly from it; but it is necessary for me to fly to
thee, that thou mayst support me under it, and make it
instrumental to my good. I am in deep distress, and my
heart faints and sinks under the burden of its sorrows.
Dearest Father, encompassed thus with danger, and
oppressed with fear, what shall I say? O save me from
this hour! But for this cause came I unto this hour, that,
after being perfectly humbled, thou mightest have the
glory of my deliverance. Be pleased, O Lord, to deliver
me! Poor and helpless as I am, what can I do, and
whither shall I go, without thee? O fortify me under this
new distress; be thou my strength and my support; and
whatever be its weight, whatever its continuance, I will
not fear.

Lord, thy will be done! This tribulation and
anguish I accept as my due: O that I may bear it with
patience till the dark storm be overpast, and light and

peace succeed! Yet thy omnipotent arm, O God, my mercy! as it hath often done before, can remove even this trial from me, or so graciously mitigate its severity that I shall not utterly sink under it. Though difficult it seems to me, how easy to thee is this change of thy right hand, O Most High!

THOMAS À KEMPIS.

Lord of all created things, my God, my Blessedness: How long must I yet wait before thou dost show thyself to me? How can one who has naught on earth find life apart from thee? How tedious and how full of sufferings is such a life in which one does really not live but experiences on every side utter abandonment, utter desolation! How long, O Lord, ah, how long will it yet last? What must I do, my Highest Good? Must I desire, really, never to yearn for thee?

My God and my Creator: thou dost wound, but thou dost offer also the healing's means. Thou dost wound, yet there can be seen no wound. Thou slayest, and thou grantest life anew. In thy omnipotence, according to thy good will, thou disposest, O Lord, of all.

Dost thou, my God, then will that I should endure such tribulation? So be it, then, my God, since thou dost will it, for my will is other, none, than thine. But oh, my Creator! the excess of my pain drives me to cry out and bewail my helplessness: thy good pleasure it be to relieve me.

The fettered soul yearns for freedom, but wills it no sooner than to thee is pleasing. My soul: let then the will of God be accomplished in thee: alone, that concerns thee. Serve the Lord, trust in his Mercy: this will soothe thy pains.

O my God, my King!—I naught can do, unless thy
mighty hand, unless thy heavenly power, assist me.

With thine aid, I can do all.

SAINT THERESA OF AVILA

❦

Almighty God, have mercy upon us, who, when
troubled with the things that are past, lose faith, and life,
and courage, and hope. So have mercy upon us, and
uphold us, that we, being sustained by a true faith that
thou art merciful and forgiving, may go on in the life of
the future to keep thy commandments, to rejoice in thy
bounty, to trust in thy mercy, and to hope in the eternal
life. Grant unto all of us, whatsoever may betide us, to
remember ever, that it is all of thy guidance, under thy
care, by thy will; that so, in darkest days, beholding thee,
we may have courage to go on, faith to endure, patience
to bear, and hopefulness to hold out, even unto the end.

GEORGE DAWSON

❦

Lead, kindly Light, amid the encircling gloom,
Lead thou me on;
The night is dark, and I am far from home;
Lead thou me on.
Keep thou my feet; I do not ask to see
The distant scene; one step enough for me.

I was not ever thus, nor prayed that thou
Shouldst lead me on;
I loved to choose and see my path; but now

Lead thou me on.
I loved the garish day, and, spite of fears,
Pride ruled my will: remember not past years.

So long thy power hath blest me, sure it still
Will lead me on
O'er moor and fen, o'er crag and torrent, till
The night is gone,
And with the morn those angel faces smile
Which I have loved long since, and lost awhile.

JOHN HENRY NEWMAN

Say not the struggle naught availeth,
The labor and the wounds are vain,
The enemy faints not, nor faileth,
And as things have been they remain.

If hopes were dupes, fears may be liars;
It may be, in yon smoke conceal'd,
Your comrades chase e'en now the fliers,
And, but for you, possess the field.

For while the tired waves, vainly breaking,
Seem here no painful inch to gain,
Far back, through creeks and inlets making,
Comes silent, flooding in, the main.

And not by eastern windows only,
When daylight comes, comes in the light,
In front, the sun climbs slow, how slowly,
But westward, look, the land is bright.

ARTHUR HUGH CLOUGH

Almighty and merciful God, we lift up our hearts to thee for all who are the prey of anxious fears, who cannot get their minds off themselves, and to whom every demand brings the feeling that they cannot cope with what is required of them. Give them the comfort of knowing that this is illness, not cowardice; that millions have felt as they feel; that there is a way through this dark valley, and light at the end of it. Lead them to those who can show them the pathway to health and happiness. Sustain them by the knowledge that the Savior knows and understands all our woe and fear; and give them enough courage to face each day, and to rest their minds in the thought that thou wilt see them through.

LESLIE D. WEATHERHEAD

2

....

I Cried unto Thee

Miracles—the lame walk, the mute speak, the deaf hear. Sherlock Holmes had a theory: when you exclude all reasonable solutions to a problem, the final answer to a mystery, no matter how impossible or improbable, must be the answer.

It requires little on our part—not belief, not faith, not trust—only openness to explore a new type of relationship.

The ancient Hebrews doubted the existence of a Promised Land when they walked for forty years in the desert. And when Jacob wrestled with his angel, he couldn't have known he would be given a new name. But they risked a new relationship, and because of it became new people.

O Lord my God, I cried unto thee, and thou hast healed me. O Lord, thou hast brought up my soul from the grave: thou hast kept me alive, that I should not go down to the pit. Sing unto the Lord, O ye saints of his, and give thanks at the remembrance of his holiness. For his anger endureth but a moment; in his favor is life: weeping may endure for a night, but joy cometh in the morning. And in my prosperity I said, I shall never be moved. Lord, by thy favor thou hast made my mountain to stand strong: thou didst hide thy face, and I was troubled. I cried to thee, O Lord; and unto the Lord I made supplication. What profit is there in my blood, when I go down to the pit? Shall the dust praise thee? Shall it declare thy truth? Hear, O Lord, and have mercy upon me: Lord, be thou my helper. Thou hast turned for me my mourning into dancing: thou hast put off my sackcloth, and girded me with gladness; to the end that my glory may sing praise to thee, and not be silent. O Lord my God, I will give thanks unto thee forever.

PSALM 30

Lord, if thou art not present, where shall I seek thee absent? If everywhere, why do I not see thee present? Thou dwellest in light inaccessible; and where is that inaccessible light? or how shall I have access to light inaccessible? I beseech thee, Lord, teach me to seek thee, and show thyself to the seeker; because I can neither seek thee, unless thou teach me, nor find thee, unless thou show thyself to me: let me seek thee in desiring thee, and desire thee in seeking thee: let me find thee in loving thee, and love thee in finding thee.

SAINT ANSELM

Thou hast made me, And shall thy worke decay?
Repaire me now, for now mine end doth haste,
I runne to death, and death meets me as fast,
And all my pleasures are like yesterday;
I dare not move my dimme eyes any way,
Despaire behind, and death before doth cast
Such terrour, and my feeble flesh doth waste
By sinne in it, which it t'wards hell doth weigh;
Onely thou art above, and when toward thee
By thy leave I can looke, I rise again;
But our old subtle foe so tempteth me,
That not one houre my selfe I can sustaine;
Thy Grace may wing me to prevent his art,
And thou like Adamant draw mine iron heart.

JOHN DONNE

To thee, the God of truth, of light and of love, to thee I speak, thou who art highest and holiest and noblest. I know that there is bad about me; when thou seest it, forget. I am like others of mine own people—of the spirits we were afraid. Our chief thought was to get food and fur to make our bodies comfortable. In this we were like the beasts—they want only a warm place in which to lie down with a full stomach.

From the beginning we lived in fear, in ignorance, and in darkness, but now from afar we see light arising; but alas! in the faint light we see the filth of our lives.

We understand that thou art our great father whose heart is filled with love for us; that thou dost love all truth and mercy and light and cleanness and goodness, and that thou dost hate the false and the dark and the cruel and the dirty and the bad. So we pray—make the light brighter that we may see more clearly and learn more of thee. Cause us to hate that which thou dost hate and to love that which thou dost love.

Father, I and my people will be strong for thee; we will fight against the bad; we will fight for the good; we will use our heads and our hearts and our hands and our feet and our tongues and all that we have to follow the truth to gratify and please thee.

ESKIMO PRAYER

Great God! what then is man, thus to wrestle during his whole life, against himself, to wish to be happy without thee, in spite of thee, in declaring himself against thee? To feel his wretchedness and yet to love it, to know his true happiness and yet to fly from it? What is man, O my God, and who shall fathom his ways and the eternal contradiction of his errors? Delivered up to his own understanding, he is continually deceived, and nothing appears to his eyes but under fictitious colors; he but imperfectly knows thee; he hardly knows himself; he comprehends nothing in all that surrounds him; he takes darkness for light; he wanders from error to error; he quits not his errors when he returns to himself. The lights alone of thy faith can direct his judgments, open the eyes of his soul, become the reason of his heart, teach him to know himself, lay open the folds of self-love, expose all the artifices of the passions, and exalt him to the spiritual man, who conceives and judges of all.

O my God! I know only too well that the world and its pleasures make none happy! Come, then, and resume thine influence over a heart which in vain endeavors to fly from thee; and which its own disgusts recall to thee in spite of itself; come to be its Redeemer, its Peace, its Light, and pay more regard to its wretchedness than to its crimes.

MASSILLON

Lord, make me see thy glory in every place:
If mortal beauty sets my heart aglow,
Shall not that earthly fire by thine burn low
Extinguished by the great light of thy grace?

Dear Lord, I cry to thee for help, O raise
Me from the misery of this blind woe,
Thy spirit alone can save me: let it flow
Through will and sense, redeeming what is base.

Thou hast given me on earth this godlike soul,
And a poor prisoner of it thou hast made
Behind weak flesh-walls; from that wretched state

How can I rescue it, how my true life find?
All goodness, Lord, must fail without thy aid:
For thou alone hast power to alter fate.

MICHELANGELO

❧

O Lord, our only Savior, we cannot bear alone our load
of responsibility; up-bear us under it. We look without
seeing unless thou purge our sight; grant us sight. We
read without comprehending, unless thou open our
understanding; give us intelligence. Nothing can we do
unless thou prosper the work of our hands upon us; "O
prosper thou our handiwork." We are weak; out of
weakness make us strong. We are in peril of death; come
and heal us. We believe; help thou our unbelief. We
hope; let us not be disappointed of our hope. We love;
grant us to love much, to love ever more and more, to
love all, and most of all to love thee. Grant this, we
humbly beseech thee.

CHRISTINA G. ROSSETTI

❧

Almighty God, whose laws are our guide, and in whose
love is our peace, we turn to thee from the perplexities
and uncertainties which daily beset us, and pray for relief
from disquieting and cowardly fears. We are bewildered
by the confusions of the world; we lose the way of
certitude and self-control; we are tempted by petty
annoyances, by despondency and doubt; the fear to do
wrong paralyzes the power to do right, and our decisions
falter under the strain of apprehension and self-distrust.
The Scripture is fulfilled in us: our hearts fail from fear,
and from looking after the things which are to come.

Restore to lives thus smitten with spiritual
prostration the sanity and courage they sorely need; and
banish the evil spirit of fear by the expulsive power of
new affections and desires. Turn our minds from

self-scrutiny to self-forgetfulness, and from the fear of doing wrong to the love of doing right. Rescue us from anticipated or imaginary troubles, that we be not anxious for the morrow, but let the morrow care for the things of itself. Assure us that surrender to fear is practical atheism, and that the trivial vicissitudes of life are forms of discipline which invite to mastery. Give us the exhilaration of moral victory, and teach us that there is no fear in love, for perfect love casteth out fear.

And through this conquest of fear by self-forgetfulness, lead our anxious hearts to the deeper meaning of experience, and to that form of fear which is justified and salutary—the fear of thy judgments, which is the beginning of our wisdom. Free us from the apprehensions which concern ourselves by the restraining fear of infidelity toward thee, and subdue our imagined ills by real and controlling faith; that we may be led from restlessness and helplessness to tranquility and strength, as those to whom thou hast given, not the spirit of fear, but of power, and of love, and of a sound mind.

FRANCIS GREENWOOD PEABODY

Almighty God, who are the only source of health and healing, the spirit of calm and central peace of the universe: grant to us, thy children, such a consciousness of thy indwelling presence as may give us utter confidence in thee. In all pain and weariness and anxiety may we throw ourselves upon thy besetting care, that knowing ourselves fenced about by thy loving omnipotence, we may permit thee to give us health and strength and peace.

JAMES THAYER ADDISON

O World invisible, we view thee,
O World intangible, we touch thee,
O World unknowable, we know thee,
Inapprehensible, we clutch thee!

Does the fish soar to find the ocean,
The eagle plunge to find the air—
That we ask of the stars in motion
If they have rumor of thee there?

Not where the wheeling systems darken,
And our benumbed conceiving soars!—
The drift of pinions, would we hearken,
Beats at our own clay-shuttered doors.

The angels keep their ancient places;
Turn but a stone, and start a wing!
'Tis ye, 'tis your estranged faces,
That miss the many-splendored thing.

But (when so sad thou canst not sadder)
Cry; and upon thy so sore loss
Shall shine the traffic of Jacob's ladder
Pitched betwixt Heaven and Charing Cross.

Yea, in the night, my soul, my daughter,
Cry, clinging Heaven by the hems;
And lo, Christ walking on the water,
Not of Gennesareth, but Thames!

FRANCIS THOMPSON

Our loving heavenly Father, no night is too dark for
thee. No pain or anguish findeth thee indifferent. Let us
place our troubled souls in thy dear enfolding arms. Let
us, in our woe, rest upon thy bosom. Spread the pinions
of thy love over our pain, that our pain itself may
become hallowed and that our endurance may become
glorified because we suffer in thee.

JEWISH PRAYER

O Lord, by all thy dealings with us, whether of joy or
pain, of light or darkness, let us be brought to thee. May
we value no treatment of us simply because it makes us
happy or because it makes us sad, because it gives or
denies what we want, but may all that thou sendest us
draw us to thee; that knowing thy loving wisdom, we
may be sure in every disappointment that thou art still
caring for us, in every darkness that thou art
enlightening us, and in every enforced idleness that thou
art still using us: yea, in every death giving us life.

PHILLIPS BROOKS

3

....

The Lord Is My Shepherd

Amazing, Grace. The child fights his parent who wants to put him in a snowsuit on a winter's day. Finally, the child gives up, and on venturing outside is secure in the warmth of the suit. Cared for not by one's own demands but by the willingness to try another way. Amazing, Grace.

God's love is relentless, excessive, unceasing, reliable. The assurance of God's love is that no matter what demons and angels of our character and relationships we will confront in the future, we will be cared for with a loving-kindness beyond our ability to imagine.

✻

The Lord is my shepherd; I shall not want. He maketh me to lie down in green pastures: he leadeth me beside the still waters. He restoreth my soul: he leadeth me in the paths of righteousness for his name's sake. Yea, though I walk through the valley of the shadow of death, I will fear no evil: for thou art with me; thy rod and thy staff they comfort me. Thou preparest a table before me in the presence of mine enemies: thou anointest my head with oil; my cup runneth over. Surely goodness and mercy shall follow me all the days of my life: and I will dwell in the house of the Lord forever.

PSALM 23

✻

Our Father which art in Heaven, hallowed be thy name. Thy kingdom come. Thy will be done in earth, as it is in Heaven. Give us this day our daily bread. And forgive us our debts, as we forgive our debtors. And lead us not into temptation, but deliver us from evil: For thine is the kingdom, and the power, and the glory, forever.

THE LORD'S PRAYER

✻

The prayers I make will then be sweet indeed
If thou the spirit give by which I pray;
My unassisted heart is barren clay,

That of its native self can nothing feed:
Of good and pious works thou art the seed
That quickens only where thou sayest it may.
Unless thou show to us thine own true way,
No man can find it. Father, thou must lead:
Do thou then breathe those thoughts into my mind
By which such virtue may in me be bred
That in thy holy footsteps I may tread;
The fetters of my tongue do thou unbind
That I may have the power to sing of thee
And sound thy praises everlastingly.

MICHELANGELO

✳

Take, O Lord, and receive my entire liberty, my
memory, my understanding, and my whole will. All that
I am, all that I have, thou hast given me, and I will give
it back again to thee to be disposed of according to thy
good pleasure. Give me only thy love and thy grace;
with thee I am rich enough, nor do I ask for aught
besides. Amen.

SAINT IGNATIUS LOYOLA

✳

Dark Angel, with thine aching lust
To rid the world of penitence:
Malicious Angel, who still dost
My soul such subtile violence!

Because of thee, no thought, no thing,
Abides for me undesecrate:
Dark Angel, ever on the wing,
Who never reachest me too late!

When music sounds, then changest thou
Its silvery to a sultry fire:
Nor will thine envious heart allow
Delight untortured by desire.

Through thee, the gracious Muses turn
To Furies, O mine Enemy!
And all the things of beauty burn
With flames of evil ecstasy.

Because of thee, the land of dreams
Becomes a gathering place of fears:
Until tormented slumber seems
One vehemence of useless tears.

When sunlight glows upon the flowers,
Or ripples down the dancing sea:
Thou, with thy troop of passionate powers,
Beleaguerest, bewilderest, me.

Within the breath of autumn woods,
Within the winter silences:
Thy venomous spirit stirs and broods,
O Master of impieties!

The ardor of red flame is thine,
And thine the steely soul of ice:
Thou poisonest the fair design
Of nature, with unfair device.

Apples of ashes, golden bright;
Waters of bitterness, how sweet!
O banquet of a foul delight,
Prepared by thee, dark Paraclete!

Thou art the whisper in the gloom,
The hinting tone, the haunting laugh:
Thou art the adorner of my tomb,
The minstrel of mine epitaph.

I fight thee, in the Holy Name!
Yet, what thou dost, is what God saith:
Tempter! should I escape thy flame,
Thou wilt have helped my soul from Death:

The second Death, that never dies,
That cannot die, when time is dead:
Live Death, wherein the lost soul cries,
Eternally uncomforted.

Dark Angel, with thine aching lust!
Of two defeats, of two despairs:
Less dread, a change to drifting dust,
Than thine eternity of cares.

Do what thou wilt, thou shalt not so,
Dark Angel! triumph over me:
Lonely, unto the Lone I go;
Divine, to the Divinity.

LIONEL JOHNSON

Lord, my heart is made bitter by its desolation: sweeten thou it, I beseech thee, with thy consolation. Lord, in hunger I began to seek thee; I beseech thee that I may not cease to hunger for thee. In hunger I have come to thee; let me not go unfed. I have come in poverty to the rich, in misery to the compassionate; let me not return empty and despised.

Teach me to seek thee and reveal thyself to me when I seek thee, for I cannot seek thee except thou teach me, nor find thee except thou reveal thyself. Let me seek thee in longing, let me long for thee in seeking; let me find thee in love, and love thee in finding. Lord, I acknowledge and I thank thee that thou hast created me in this thine image in order that I may be mindful of thee, may conceive of thee, and love thee; but that image has been so consumed and wasted away by vices and obscured by the smoke of wrongdoing that it cannot achieve that for which it was made except thou renew it and create it anew. I do not endeavor, O Lord, to penetrate thy sublimity, for in no wise do I compare my understanding with that; but I long to understand in some degree thy truth, which my heart believes and loves.

Is the eye of the soul darkened by its infirmity, or dazzled by thy glory? Surely it is both darkened in itself and dazzled by thee.

Truly, O Lord, this is the unapproachable light in which thou dwellest; for truly there is nothing else which can penetrate this light, that it may see thee there. Truly, I see it not, because it is too bright for me. And yet, whatever I see, I see through it, as the weak eye sees what it sees through the light of the sun, which in the sun itself it cannot look upon.

O Supreme and Unapproachable Light! O Whole
and Blessed Truth, how far art thou from me, who am
so near to thee! How far art thou removed from my
vision, though I am so near to thine! Everywhere thou
art wholly present, and I see thee not. In thee I move,
and in thee I have my being, and I cannot come to thee:
thou art within me, and about me, and I feel thee not.

SAINT ANSELM

O Lord, grant us to love thee; grant that we may love
those that love thee; grant that we may do the deeds that
win thy love. Make the love of thee to be dearer to us
than ourselves, than our families, than wealth, and even
than cool water.

MOHAMMED

Lord, thou knowest what is best for me to do, according
to thy will. Give me, I beseech thee, what thou wilt, as
much as thou wilt, and when thou wilt. Do with me as
thou knowest best to be done, and as it shall please thee,
and as may be most for thy honor; put me where thou
wilt, and freely do with me in all things after thy will
and pleasure. I am thy creature, and in thy hands: lead
me, O God, and turn me wheresoever thou wilt. Lo! I
am thy servant, ready to do all things that thou
commandest me; for I desire not to live to myself, but to
thee.

BISHOP HICKES

❧

Lord, grant us a childlike trust in thee. What the day
will bring forth we know not. Futile alike are our hopes
and fears. We can be sure of thee alone. We rest in thee,
O Father, and resting in thee, our step is firm, our path
secure.

JEWISH PRAYER

❧

I have found you in so many places, Lord. I have felt
your heartbeat in the perfect stillness of the open fields,
in the shadowy tabernacle of an empty cathedral, in the
oneness of heart and mind of an assembly of people who
love you and fill the arches of your church with hymns
and with love.

I have found you in joy. I search for you and often
I find you. But in suffering I always find you. Suffering
of any kind is like the sound of the bell summoning
God's bride to prayer.

When the shadow of the cross appears, the soul
recollects itself inwardly and, forgetful of the sound of
the bell, it "sees" you and speaks with you.

It is you who come to visit me and I answer you,
"Here I am, Lord. I have looked for you. I have longed
for you. . . ." In this meeting the soul no longer feels its
suffering but seems to be enraptured with your love,
completely filled by you, suffused with you. I in you and
you in me, that we may be one.

Then once again I open my eyes to life, a life less
real now that I am divinely strengthened to follow your
way.

Lord, I have found you in the terrible magnitude of

the suffering of others. I have seen you in the sublime
acceptance and unaccountable joy of those whose lives
are racked with pain, and I have heard your voice in the
words of those whose personal agony mysteriously
increases their selfless concern for other people.

But in my own niggling aches and petty sorrows I
have failed to find you. I have lost the drama of your
great redemptive passion in my own mundane weariness
and the joyful life . . . is submerged in the drabness of
self-preoccupation.

Lord, I believe. Help thou my unbelief.

MOTHER TERESA

Lord, we know not what we ought to ask of thee; thou
only knowest what we need; thou lovest us better than
we know how to love ourselves. O Father! give to us,
thy children, that which we ourselves know not how to
ask. We would have no other desire than to accomplish
thy will. Teach us to pray. Pray thyself in us.

FRANÇOIS DE LA MOTHE FÉNELON

This is our prayer to thee, our Lord; strike, strike at the
root of penury in our hearts.

Give us the strength lightly to bear our joys and
sorrows.

Give us the strength to make our love fruitful in
service.

Give us the strength never to disown the poor or
bend our knees before insolent might.

Give us the strength to raise our minds high above
daily trifles.

And give us the strength to surrender our strength
to thy will with love.

RABINDRANATH TAGORE

Abide with me; fast falls the eventide;
The darkness deepens; Lord, with me abide;
When other helpers fail, and comforts flee,
Help of the helpless, oh abide with me.

Swift to its close ebbs out life's little day;
Earth's joys grow dim, its glories pass away;
Change and decay in all around I see;
O Thou who changest not, abide with me.

I need thy presence every passing hour;
What but thy grace can foil the tempter's power?
Who like thyself my guide and stay can be?
Through cloud and sunshine, Lord, abide with me.

I fear no foe with thee at hand to bless;
Ills have no weight, and tears no bitterness;
Where is death's sting? where, grave, thy victory?
I triumph still, if thou abide with me.

Hold then thy cross before my closing eyes;
Shine through the gloom, and point me to the skies;
Heaven's morning breaks, and earth's vain shadows
    flee;
In life, in death, O Lord, abide with me.

HENRY FRANCIS LYTE

4

....

Why Boast in Mischief?

Jacob didn't know who he was wrestling with, or what the outcome would be. But he knew he had to wrestle.

We are at the point where we must go forward because we can't go back. We are assured of God's love. The prospects, though, are fearful. Yet, the news will be heartening if we discover that we are capable of developing a loving relationship with the most important person in our life, the person who will be with us always—ourselves.

When he spoke of the devout life, St. Francis de Sales encouraged an examination of conscience not as a method of self-abasement, but as a means to live a free and productive life. When we are able to define who we are, and see what our core values have been, then we are in a position to hold to that which is dear and change that which is not.

❧

Why boastest thou thyself in mischief, O mighty man?
The goodness of God endureth continually. Thy tongue
deviseth mischiefs; like a sharp razor, working deceitfully.
Thou lovest evil more than good; and lying rather than
to speak righteousness. Thou lovest all devouring words,
O thou deceitful tongue. God shall likewise destroy thee
forever, he shall take thee away, and pluck thee out of
thy dwelling place, and root thee out of the land of the
living. The righteous also shall see, and fear, and shall
laugh at him: Lo, this is the man that made not God his
strength; but trusted in the abundance of his riches, and
strengthened himself in his wickedness. But I am like a
green olive tree in the house of God: I trust in the
mercy of God forever and ever. I will praise thee
forever, because thou hast done it: and I will wait on thy
name; for it is good before thy saints.

PSALM 52

❧

May the Lord give us both the honesty and strength to
look our own faults squarely in the face and not ever
continue to excuse and minimize them, while they grow.
Grant us that wide view of ourselves which our
neighbors possess, or better the highest view of infinite
justice and goodness and efficiency. In that great white
light let us see the littleness and narrowness of our souls
and the deeds of our days, and then forthwith begin their

betterment. Only thus shall we broaden out of the vicious circle of our own admiration into the greater commendation of God.

W. E. B. DuBois

Batter my heart, three person'd God; for, you
As yet but knocke, breathe, shine, and seeke to
    mend,
That I may rise, and stand, o'erthrow mee, and
    bend
Your force, to breake, blowe, burn, and make me
    new.
I, like an usurpt towne, to'another due,
Labor to'admit you, but oh, to no end,
Reason your viceroy in mee, mee should defend,
But is captiv'd, and proves weake or untrue.
Yet dearely I love you, and would be loved faine,
But am bethroth'd unto your enemie:
Divorce mee, untie, or breake that knot againe,
Take mee to you, imprison mee, for I
Except you'enthrall mee, never shall be free,
Nor ever chast, except you ravish mee.

JOHN DONNE

O Lord, in whose hands are life and death, by whose power I am sustained, and by whose mercy I am spared, look down upon me with pity. Forgive me that I have until now so much neglected the duty which thou hast assigned to me, and suffered the days and hours to pass away without any endeavor to accomplish thy will. Make me to remember, O God, that every day is thy gift and ought to be used according to thy command. Grant me, therefore, so to repent of my negligence, that I may obtain mercy from thee and pass the time which thou shalt yet allow me in diligent performance of thy commands.

SAMUEL JOHNSON

Have I penitence, grief, shame,
pain, honor, weariness for my sin?
Do I pray, if not seven times, as David,
yet at least thrice, as Daniel?
If not, as Solomon, at length,
yet shortly, as the Publican?
If not, like Christ, the whole night,
at least for one hour?
If not on the ground, and in ashes,
at least not in my bed?
If not in sackcloth,
at least not in purple and fine linen?
If not altogether freed from all,
at least from immoderate desires?
Do I give, if not, as Zaccheus, fourfold,
at least, as the law commands, with the fifth
part added?
If not as the rich,
yet as the widow?
If not the half,
yet the thirtieth part?
If not above my power,
yet up to my power?

LANCELOT ANDREWS

43

𖤣

When my mind is burnt by contact with the fire of
hatred, that fire immediately should be extinguished, out
of fear that one's merit may be consumed.

If one who is to die is saved by cutting off a hand,
why is he unfortunate? If one is saved from hell by
human sorrows, why is he unfortunate?

If today one is not able to suffer even this measure
of sorrow, why is anger, the cause of pain in hell, not
restrained?

By reason of anger, I have been oppressed in hell
thousands of times, and what I have done has been
neither to my benefit nor to the benefit of others.

This is not such a sorrow, and it will create great
benefit. One should be glad of the sorrow which takes
away the sorrow of the world.

If joy and happiness are obtained by praising the
good qualities of others, why, O mind, are you not
gratified? Here is delight and happiness for you, an
upswelling of pleasure without reproach, and it is not
forbidden. Because of these good qualities, this is the best
way of attracting others.

BUDDHIST PRAYER

𖤣

From foolish thoughts and false affections,
Good Lord, deliver us.

From anger and passion, from suspicion and envy,
from harsh judgment and evil-speaking, from
uncharitable thought, and from all impatience,
Good Lord, deliver us.

From acquiescence in our faults, and from fruitless
sorrow because of them,

Good Lord, deliver us.

From all murmuring at our lot, or repining because of the burdens laid upon us,
Good Lord, deliver us.

From putting darkness for light, and light for darkness; from calling evil good, and good evil; from resisting thy Spirit, and yielding to temptation,
Good Lord, deliver us.

From giving and from taking offense; from timidity and rashness; from self-assertion, and from following the multitude,
Good Lord, deliver us.

From evil thoughts, and low desires,
Good Lord, deliver us.

From covetousness, vainglory, and sloth,
Good Lord, deliver us.

From envy, malice, and all uncharitableness,
Good Lord, deliver us.

From revenge, and the remembrance of injuries,
Good Lord, deliver us.

From self-love, and the forgetfulness of benefits,
Good Lord, deliver us.

BOOK OF COMMON PRAYER

O Father, just as we look into a mirror to see any soiled spots on our face, so let us look to thee in order to understand the things which we have done amiss. We are like a reed shaken in the wind; we are inexpressibly weak, leave us not to ourselves, but dwell in our hearts and guide our thoughts and actions.

KOREAN PRAYER

Eternal Spirit, thou dwellest in light unapproachable,
beyond the power of our thought to comprehend or our
imagination to portray. Yet thou art revealed to us in the
order of the world we live in, in the truth our minds
discover, in the inward presence of thy Spirit, and above
all in Christ, thy Son. With reverent hearts we worship
thee.

We would bring our fragmentary lives into the
presence of thy wholeness. We would bring our transient
thoughts into the light of thine eternity. We would bring
our restless spirits into the calm strength of thine
everlasting purpose.

See what complaints we have brought into thy
sanctuary against the circumstances that have fretted us,
against the human friends who have failed us, against the
enemies who have wronged us, and even against the justice
of thine order that has hurt us. Teach us, nevertheless,
we beseech thee, to search our own lives, to see that each
man is his own destiny, that each soul is its own heaven
and its own hell. Send us back into our own souls to
find there by thy grace, peace and power, and adequacy
to conquer life. May we be victors and not victims.

O God, we would escape from ourselves this hour,
from our little and partial selves, from our mean and
selfish selves. We would escape from our fragmentary
and broken selves into thy greatness. Teach us once
again the everlasting mystery that only as we lose
ourselves in something higher than ourselves can we find
ourselves.

To this end give us a great faith to live by. From
doubt and disillusionment, from cynicism and rebellion,
deliver us, good Lord. For uncertainty give us
confidence. Though we may not see all things clearly, let

us see some great things plainly that we may live by them. O God, give us light enough to walk by.

Give us wisdom to live by, we beseech thee. We who walk so often blindly through the tortuous labyrinth of life, give us a clue this day. Let us have vision to see the way we ought to take through some perplexing circumstance. Let high decisions be made on the right side of great questions in thy sanctuary.

Give us love to live by, we pray thee. Enlarge our sympathies; deepen our understandings and compassions. Save us from resentfulness. Cast down within us pettiness and meanness, and lift us up to largeness of mind and heart that we may have the grace to take within the compass of our care those whom by prejudice we have shut out or through dislike have hurt.

Give us great causes to live for. O God, we thank thee for this difficult and serious time, this generation of many dangers and many open doors. Save us from living on a small scale in a great age. Open the eyes of some youths here to causes worth giving life to, that they may be glorified, not alone by what they are, but by what they identify themselves with. Lift us up into better days in the nation. Build justice into our economic order. Grant vision and courage to our statesmen. Make us equal to our international responsibilities and opportunities. And grant that we all may play a part in the things that matter most in our time, so that we may leave this world a fairer home for thy family.

HARRY EMERSON FOSDICK

O Father in Heaven, who didst fashion my limbs to serve thee and my soul to follow hard after thee, with sorrow and contrition of heart I acknowledge before thee

the faults and failures of the day that is now past. Too
long, O Father, have I tried thy patience; too often have
I betrayed the sacred trust thou hast given me to keep;
yet thou art still willing that I should come to thee in lowli-
ness of heart, as now I do, beseeching thee to drown
my transgressions in the sea of thine own infinite love.

> My failure to be true even to my own accepted
> standards:
> My self-deception in face of temptation:
> My choosing of the worse when I know the better:
> O Lord, forgive.
> My failure to apply to myself the standards of
> conduct I demand of others:
> My blindness to the suffering of others and my
> slowness to be taught by my own:
> My complacence toward wrongs that do not touch
> my own case and my oversensitiveness to those
> that do:
> My slowness to see the good in my fellows and to
> see the evil in myself:
> My hardness of heart toward my neighbors' faults
> and my readiness to make allowance for my own:
> My unwillingness to believe that thou hast called
> me to a small work and my brother to a greater
> one: O Lord, forgive.

JOHN BAILLIE

O God, who art of great kindness, remove far from us all
occasions and effects of anger. Give us mild, peaceable,
meek, and humble spirits, that, remembering our own
infirmities, we may bear with those of others; that we
may think lowlily of ourselves, and not be angry when

others also think lowlily of us; that we may be patient
toward all men, gentle and easy to be entreated; as God
is so to us.

THOMAS WILSON

Lord, there are many such,
Dwelling in narrow resentments,
Embittered by wrongs that others have inflicted,
Confined to harsh enmities,
Imprisoned in spirit by despair at evil deeds,
Drained of hope and bereft of peace,
Left to great hatred in this world.

Have mercy, good Lord, upon all these
Whose world, through human malice,
Despairs of human kindness.

Judge and turn their oppressors.
Release again, for the fearful,
The springs of trust and goodness.
Give them liberty of heart
The liberty of those who leave room
For the judgment of God.

Enlarge our hearts, O God,
That we may do battle against evil
And bear the sorrows of the weary,
And seek and serve thy will.
Great art thou, O Lord.
There is naught that is a match for thee. Amen.

O my Lord, enlarge my heart.

SURAH OF TĀ HĀ

5

....

Have Mercy on Me

Carl Jung noted that there is no secret worthy of the name. We are entitled to be free of the emotional blackmail that we so often impose on ourselves in the isolation and fearfulness of secretiveness.

When we drag our secrets into the light of day, they cease to dominate and drive us. The process also forces us to give up the arrogant notion of our uniqueness, and thus our estrangement from the rest of humankind.

Over time we discover that God forgives. We also learn the value of forgiving others. But accepting ourselves is especially hard. Here is where God's love gives us the strength to move beyond our past and into the future. Here is where all things are made new.

Have mercy upon me, O God, according to thy
loving-kindness: according unto the multitude of thy
tender mercies blot out my transgressions. Wash me
thoroughly from mine iniquity, and cleanse me from my
sin. For I acknowledge my transgressions: and my sin is
ever before me. Against thee, thee only, have I sinned,
and done this evil in thy sight: that thou mightest be
justified when thou speakest, and be clear when thou
judgest. Behold, I was shapen in iniquity; and in sin did
my mother conceive me. Behold, thou desirest truth in
the inward parts: and in the hidden part thou shalt make
me to know wisdom. Purge me with hyssop, and I shall
be clean: wash me, and I shall be whiter than snow.
Make me to hear joy and gladness; that the bones which
thou hast broken may rejoice. Hide thy face from my
sins, and blot out all mine iniquities. Create in me a clean
heart, O God; and renew a right spirit within me. Cast
me not away from thy presence; and take not thy holy
spirit from me. Restore unto me the joy of thy salvation;
and uphold me with thy free spirit. Then will I teach
transgressors thy ways; and sinners shall be converted
unto thee. Deliver me from blood guiltiness, O God,
thou God of my salvation: and my tongue shall sing
aloud of thy righteousness. O Lord, open thou my lips;
and my mouth shall shew forth thy praise. For thou
desirest not sacrifice; else would I give it: thou delightest
not in burnt offering. The sacrifices of God are a broken

spirit: a broken and a contrite heart, O God, thou wilt
not despise. Do good in thy good pleasure unto Zion:
build thou the walls of Jerusalem. Then shalt thou be
pleased with the sacrifices of righteousness, with burnt
offering and whole burnt offering: then shall they offer
bullocks upon thine altar.

PSALM 51

🌿

Almighty God, Father of our Lord Jesus Christ, we
humbly acknowledge our manifold sins and offenses
against thee by thought and deed. We have neglected
opportunities of good which thou in thy love gavest unto
us. We have been overcome by temptations, from which
thou wast ready to guard us. We have looked unto men,
and not unto thee, in doing our daily work. We have
thought too little of others, and too much of our own
pleasure, in all our plans. We have lived in forgetfulness
of the life to come. But thou art ever merciful and
gracious to those that turn to thee. So we now come to
thee as those whom thou wilt not cast out. Hear, O
Lord, and have mercy upon us. O Almighty God,
heavenly Father, who forgivest iniquity and
transgression; O Lord Jesus Christ, Lamb of God, who
takest away the sin of the world; O Holy Spirit who
helpest the infirmities of those that pray; receive our
humble confession. Give us true repentance and sincere
faith in thee. Do away our offenses, and give us grace to
live hereafter more worthily of our Christian calling, for
the glory of thy Great Name.

BISHOP WESTCOTT

All that we ought to have thought and have not
    thought,
All that we ought to have said and have not said,
All that we ought to have done and have not done;
All that we ought not to have thought and yet have
    thought,
All that we ought not to have spoken and yet have
    spoken,
All that we ought not to have done and yet have
    done;
For thoughts, words, and works, pray we, O God,
    for forgiveness.
And repent with penance.

ZOROASTER, THE ZENDAVESTA

Almighty and most merciful Father, who knowest us
altogether, we confess that we have erred, and failed. We
have come short, and transgressed; we have sinned
against thee, in thought, word, and deed. We have
forsaken the fountain of living waters, and hewn out for
ourselves cisterns that hold no water. We are ashamed of
these things, and repent of our wrongdoing. We beseech
thee, O Lord, to grant us thy forgiveness, and to assure
us of it, as thou alone canst; enabling us in days to come
to amend our lives according to thy law. By thine
omnipresent Spirit, do thou incline our wills forever to
that which is right. In thy wisdom make us wise; and
grant that with our whole heart we may serve thee in
days to come.

BOOK OF COMMON PRAYER

❧

Almighty and most merciful God, the fountain of all
goodness, who knowest the thoughts of our hearts, we
confess that we have transgressed against thee. Wash us,
we beseech thee, from the stains of our past sins, and
give us grace and power to put away all hurtful things;
so that we may bring forth fruits meet for repentance.

O eternal Light, shine into our hearts; eternal
Goodness, deliver us from evil; eternal Power, be thou
our support; eternal Wisdom, scatter our ignorance;
eternal Pity, have mercy upon us. Grant that with all our
heart and mind and strength, we may evermore seek thy
face; and finally bring us, by thine infinite mercy, to thy
holy presence.

ALCUIN

❧

Thou who hast created me
by thy goodness,
let not thy work come to naught
through my iniquity.
What is thine in me acknowledge;
what is mine, take away.
Look on me, the wretched,
O boundless Loving-Kindness:
on me, the wicked,
O Compassion that extendest to all!
Infirm I come to the Almighty,
wounded I hasten to the Physician:
reserve for me the gentleness
of thy compassion,

56

Who hast so long held suspended the sword
of thy vengeance.
Blot out the number of my crimes,
renew the multitude of thy compassions.
However unclean, thou canst cleanse me;
however blind, enlighten me;
however weak, restore me;
yea, though dead, raise me.
Of what kind soever I am, be it good or bad,
I am ever thine.
If thou cast me out, who shall take me in?
If thou disregard me, who shall look on me?
More canst thou remit, than I commit;
more canst thou spare, than I offend.
Let not noxious pleasures overcome me;
at the least, let not any perverse habit overwhelm
    me.
Preserve me
from depraved and lawless desires;
from vain, hurtful, impure imaginations;
from the illusions of evil spirits;
from pollutions of soul and of body.

LANCELOT ANDREWS

Lord, I most humbly acknowledge and confesse, that I
have understood sin, by understanding thy laws and
judgments; but have done against thy known and
revealed will. Thou hast set up many candlesticks, and
kindled many lamps in mee; but I have either blown
them out, or carried them to guide me in and by
forbidden ways. Thou hast given mee a desire of

knowledge, and some meanes to it, and some possession of it; and I have arm'd my self with thy weapons against thee: Yet, O God, have mercy upon me, for thine own sake have mercy upon me. Let not sin and me be able to exceed thee, nor to defraud thee, nor to frustrate thy purposes: But let me, in despite of me, be of so much use to thy glory, that by thy mercy to my sin, other sinners may see how much sin thou canst pardon. Thus show mercy to many in one: And shew thy power and al-mightinesse upon thy self, by casting manacles upon thine own hands, and calling back those Thunder-bolts which thou hadst thrown against me. Show thy Justice upon the common Seducer and Devourer of us all: and show to us so much of thy Judgments, as may instruct, not condemn us. Hear us, O God, hear us, for this contrition which thou hast put into us, who come to thee with that watchword.

JOHN DONNE

O most merciful Father,
Thou who art ever more willing to forgive than we
    to ask,
Pardon our transgressions.
In the lonely hours of forgetfulness
We have been unmindful of thee
    and of thy commandments;
O God forgive us, we pray.
In our indifference we have been unfaithful to those
    we love,
And to him who didst open our eyes to thee,
Jesus Christ, our Lord.
As a child plays and is burned,

As a child stumbles and falls,
So we are hurt by our willfulness:
Make us whole;
Give us strong limbs for walking,
And strong wills in the places we are weak.
Reward those we have hurt,
And make us strong to reward them ourselves.
We rejoice in the warmth of thy affection
And in the peace of thy forgiveness.
To thee and to Jesus Christ, thy son,
Be honor and glory, world without end.

R.L.D.

God strengthen me to bear myself;
That heaviest weight of all to bear,
Inalienable weight of care.

All others are outside myself;
I lock my door and bar them out,
The turmoil, tedium, gad-about.

I lock my door upon myself
And bar them out; but who shall wall
Self from myself, most loathed of all?

If I could once lay down myself,
And start self-purged upon the race
That all must run! Death runs apace.

If I could set aside myself,
And start with lightened heart upon
The road by all men overgone!

God harden me against myself,
This coward with pathetic voice
Who craves for ease, and rest, and joys:

Myself, arch-traitor to myself;
My hollowest friend, my deadliest foe,
My clog whatever road I go.

Yet One there is can curb myself,
Can roll the strangling load from me,
Break off the yoke and set me free.

CHRISTINA ROSSETTI

O God I need thee
When morning crowds the night away
And the tasks of waking seize my mind—
I need thy Poise.

O God I need thee
When clashes come with those
Who walk the way with me
I need thy Smile.

O God I need thee
When love is hard to see
Amid the ugliness and slime
I need thy Eyes.

O God I need thee
When the path to take before me lies
I see it—courage flees
I need thy Faith.

O God I need thee
When the day's work is done
Tired, discouraged—wasted;
I need thy Rest.

HOWARD THURMAN

Lord, undertake for me. Quiet my selfish clamoring. Be
thou my sufficiency. All things happen according to thy
ordering. And if thou orderest my life, there can be no
room for anything but joy when thy decree goeth forth;
for thy ordering is alone secure. No planning or
scheming of mine will mar thy plan for me. Nothing
remains for me but to fit myself into thy plan. And so
shall I reach my highest good and find opportunity for
my highest, fullest service. Lord be thou my peace. Lay
hold of my faculties and train them to thy use. Inspire
me with undying devotion to thee and thy will. I am
afraid of my weakness. Let it be a vessel to hold thy
strength. Let me not break, O God. Fill me with divine
power.

CHARLES HENRY BRENT

O God,
I want to thank you
for bringing me this far along the road to recovery.
It is good to be able
to get my feet on the floor again;
It is good to be able
to do at least some things for myself again.
It is best of all

just to have the joy
of feeling well again.
O God,
keep me grateful,
grateful to all the people
who helped me back to health;
grateful to you
for the way in which
you have brought me through it all.
O God,
still give me patience.
Help me
not to be in too big a hurry to do too much.
Help me
to keep on doing what I'm told to do.
Help me
to be so obedient to those who know
what is best for me, that very soon
I shall be on the top of the world
and on the top of my job again.

I can say what the psalmist said:
I waited patiently for the Lord;
he inclined to me and heard my cry.

He took me from a fearful pit,
and from the miry clay,
And on a rock he set my feet,
establishing my way.

WILLIAM BARCLAY

6

....

I Will Extol Thee

Do you remember what it was like before you learned to ride a bicycle? You were aware you couldn't ride, yet at some point became willing to learn. While you knew the learning process wouldn't be perfect, nothing could keep you from learning. You were willing to fall and start over again and again, without a second thought.

Part of your learning had to do with finding someone who already knew how to ride—someone caring and supportive, yet able to point out where mistakes were being made. Over time, your errors decreased and your skill increased.

But remember, even in the Tour de France the best riders sometimes fall.

𐤟

I will extol thee, my God, O King; and I will bless thy name forever and ever. Every day will I bless thee; and I will praise thy name forever and ever. Great is the Lord, and greatly to be praised; and his greatness is unsearchable. One generation shall praise thy works to another, and shall declare thy mighty acts. I will speak of the glorious honor of thy majesty, and of thy wondrous works. And men shall speak of the might of thy terrible acts: and I will declare thy greatness. They shall abundantly utter the memory of thy great goodness, and shall sing of thy righteousness. The Lord is gracious, and full of compassion; slow to anger, and of great mercy. The Lord is good to all: and his tender mercies are over all his works. All thy works shall praise thee, O Lord; and thy saints shall bless thee. They shall speak of the glory of thy kingdom, and talk of thy power; to make known to the sons of men his mighty acts, and the glorious majesty of his kingdom. Thy kingdom is an everlasting kingdom, and thy dominion endureth throughout all generations. The Lord upholdeth all that fall, and raiseth up all those that be bowed down. The eyes of all wait upon thee; and thou givest them their meat in due season. Thou openest thine hand, and satisfiest the desire of every living thing. The Lord is righteous in all his ways, and holy in all his works. The Lord is nigh unto all them that call upon him, to all that call upon him in truth. He will fulfill the desire of them that fear him: he also will hear their cry, and will save them. The Lord preserveth all them that love him: but all the wicked will he destroy. My mouth shall speak the praise of the Lord: and let all flesh bless his holy name forever and ever.

PSALM 145

God, who touchest earth with beauty,
Make me lovely too;
With thy Spirit re-create me,
Make my heart anew.

Like thy springs and running waters,
Make me crystal pure;
Like thy rocks of towering grandeur
Make me strong and sure.

Like thy dancing waves in sunlight,
Make me glad and free;
Like the straightness of the pine-trees
Let me upright be.

Like the arching of the heavens,
Lift my thoughts above;
Turn my dreams to noble action—
Ministries of love.

God, who touchest earth with beauty,
Make me lovely too;
Keep me ever, by thy Spirit,
Pure and strong and true.

MARY S. EDGAR.

Justify my soul, O God, but also from your fountains fill
my will with fire. Shine in my mind, although perhaps
this means "be darkness to my experience," but occupy
my heart with your tremendous Life. Let my eyes see
nothing in the world but your glory, and let my hands
touch nothing that is not for your service. Let my
tongue taste no bread that does not strengthen me to
praise your great mercy. I will hear your voice and I will
hear all harmonies you have created, singing your
hymns. Sheep's wool and cotton from the field shall
warm me enough that I may live in your service; I will
give the rest to your poor. Let me use all things for one
sole reason: to find my joy in giving you glory.

Therefore keep me, above all things, from sin. Keep
me from the death of deadly sin which puts hell in my
soul. Keep me from the murder of lust that blinds and
poisons my heart. Keep me from the sins that eat a man's
flesh with irresistible fire until he is devoured. Keep me
from loving money in which is hatred, from avarice and
ambition that suffocate my life. Keep me from the dead
works of vanity and the thankless labor in which artists
destroy themselves for pride and money and reputation,
and saints are smothered under the avalanche of their
own importunate zeal. Stanch in me the rank wound of
covetousness and the hungers that exhaust my nature
with their bleeding. Stamp out the serpent envy that
stings love with poison and kills all joy.

Untie my hands and deliver my heart from sloth.
Set me free from the laziness that goes about disguised as
activity when activity is not required of me, and from
the cowardice that does what is not demanded, in order
to escape sacrifice.

But give me the strength that waits upon you in silence and peace. Give me humility in which alone is rest, and deliver me from pride which is the heaviest of burdens. And possess my whole heart and soul with the simplicity of love. Occupy my whole life with the one thought and the one desire of love, that I may love not for the sake of merit, not for the sake of perfection, not for the sake of virtue, not for the sake of sanctity, but for you alone.

For there is only one thing that can satisfy love and reward it, and that is you alone.

THOMAS MERTON

O God, thou hast been gracious to men and bestowed upon them a moral awareness. It is a spirit from thee. What it enjoins and what it prohibits are alike thine. Whosoever obeys it obeys thee: he who flouts it flouts thee. Thou hast left to us the obeying of it.

Keep our doings within the bounds of this moral sense. O God, do not let us be so encumbered with the things of this world that we transgress the bounds of conscience. O God, so inspire men that they follow no other guidance. Teach them not to override it for any alternative, however impressive. Let them set up no idols to its exclusion to be worshiped or esteemed as good.

For, outside conscience, there is no good. O God, guide those who preside over human affairs that they establish no order that will oblige men to transgress conscience and that they do not inflict on others wrongs that are immediate and concrete, for the sake of something supposedly and ultimately good for society. For this is the origin of man's tragic trouble and the source of the evil within him.

O God, thou hast not endowed conscience with material force to compel from man a reluctant obedience. So grant them inwardly a spiritual compulsion in which they will follow it out of choice and delight. . . . O God, guide thy servants who have gone almost irretrievably astray. Thou art the Hearer and the Answerer.

KĀMIL HUSSEIN

Give unto us, O God, we beseech thee, an unreprovable faith, a humble hope, and a never failing charity. Grant unto us true humility, a meek and quiet spirit, a loving, friendly, and useful conversation, the denying of ourselves, and the bearing of the burdens of our neighbors. Grant us the blessedness of doing good. May we be strong in purpose, diligent in duty, slow to anger, and ready for every good work.

JEREMY TAYLOR

O thou in whose boundless being are laid up all treasures of wisdom and truth and holiness, grant that through constant fellowship with thee the true graces of Christian character may more and more take shape within my soul:

The grace of a thankful and uncomplaining heart:

The grace to await thy leisure patiently and to answer thy call promptly:

The grace of courage, whether in suffering or in danger:

The grace to endure hardness as a good soldier of Jesus Christ:

The grace of boldness in standing for what is right:

69

The grace of preparedness, lest I enter into temptation:

The grace of bodily discipline:

The grace of strict truthfulness:

The grace to treat others as I would have others treat me:

The grace of charity, that I may refrain from hasty judgment:

The grace of silence, that I may refrain from hasty speech:

The grace of forgiveness toward all who have wronged me:

The grace of tenderness toward all who are weaker than myself:

The grace of steadfastness in continuing to desire that thou wilt do as now I pray.

JOHN BAILLIE

What have we, O heavenly Father, that we have not received? Every good gift, and every perfect gift, is from above, and cometh down from thee, which art the Father of lights. Seeing, then, all that we have is thine, whether it pertain to the body or the soul, how can we be proud, and boast ourselves of that which is none of our own; seeing also that as to give, so also to take away again, thou art able and wilt, whensoever thy gifts be abused, and thou not acknowledged to be the giver of them? Take, therefore, away from me all pride and haughtiness of mind, graft in me true humility, that I may acknowledge thee the giver of all good things, be thankful unto thee for them, and use them to thy glory and the profit of my neighbor. Grant also that all my glory and rejoicing may be in no earthly creatures, but in thee alone, which dost mercy, equity, and righteousness upon earth. To thee alone be all glory.

LITURGIES OF KING EDWARD VI

Ah, Lord: All that I hitherto have suffered has tended only to my destruction, marred, as it has been, by sin. But now, dear Lord, I return to thee. Thou surely wilt yet save me! Thy will shall be done. I will follow out thy designs and labor to conform my will to thine. O most sweet will of my God: Be thou forever done! Oh, that I may do thy will this day and always in every perfection! O Goodness most pleasing! be it as thou hast willed. O Eternal Will! live and reign in every will of mine and over every will of mine, now and forever.

O my God: Henceforth I resolve to strive earnestly to be patient and gentle, and not to allow the waters of contradiction to extinguish the fire of that charity which I owe to my neighbor.

SAINT FRANCIS DeSALES

O Lord of souls, in thee are the springs of my life. Abundantly give me thy Blessed Spirit, without whom nothing is strong, nothing is holy; and use me as it shall please thee for the glory of thy name. Make my will patient, my conscience pure, my temper bright. Empty me of self, and fill me with the meekness of wisdom. Increase my faith, mellow my judgment, stir my zeal, enlarge my heart. Let my life enforce what my lips utter.

Preserve me from jealousy and impatience; from self-will and depression. Make me faithful unto death and then give me the crown of life.

BISHOP A. W. THOROLD

How fresh, O Lord, how sweet and clean
Are thy returns! ev'n as the flowers in Spring,
To which, besides their own demean,
The late-past frosts tributes of pleasure bring;
    Grief melts away
    Like snow in May,
As if there were no such cold thing.

    Who would have thought my shrivel'd heart
Could have recover'd greennesse? It was gone
Quite under ground; as flow'rs depart
To see their mother-root, when they have blown;
    Where they together
    All the hard weather,
Dead to the world, keep house unknown.

    These are thy wonders, Lord of power,
Killing and quickning, bringing down to Hell
And up to Heaven in an houre;
Making a chiming of a passing-bell.
    We say amisse
    This or that is;
Thy word is all, if we could spell.

    O that I once past changing were,
Fast in thy Paradise, where no flower can wither!
Many a Spring I shoot up fair,
Offring at Heav'n, growing and groaning thither;

Nor doth my flower
Want a spring-showre,
My sinnes and I joining together.

But while I grow in a straight line,
Still upwards bent, as if Heav'n were mine own,
Thy anger comes, and I decline:
What frost to that? what pole is not the zone,
Where all things burn,
When thou dost turn,
And the least frown of thine is shown?

And now in age I bud again,
After so many deaths I live and write;
I once more smell the dew and rain,
And relish versing: O, my onely Light,
It cannot be
That I am he
On whom thy tempests fell all night.

These are thy wonders, Lord of love,
To make us see we are but flow'rs that glide;
Which when we once can finde and prove,
Thou hast a garden for us where to bide;
Who would be more,
Swelling through store,
Forfeit their Paradise by their pride.

GEORGE HERBERT

Lord, what a change within us one short hour
Spent in thy presence will avail to make—
What heavy burdens from our bosoms take,
What parched grounds refresh as with a shower!

We kneel, and all around us seems to lower;
We rise, and all, the distant and the near,
Stands forth in sunny outline, brave and clear;
We kneel, how weak; we rise, how full of power!
Why, therefore, should we do ourselves this wrong,
Or others—that we are not always strong;
That we are overborne with care,
That we should ever weak or heartless be,
Anxious or troubled, when with us is prayer,
And joy and strength and courage are with thee?

RICHARD C. TRENCH

7

....

I Will Lift Up Mine Eyes

Meister Eckhart said: "Humble the tool when praised for what the hand is doing."

Keeping things in the proper perspective is the basis of humility. Humility is neither more nor less than consistently testing reality. The ultimate reality is reliance upon God's grace, strength, and love in the conduct of our lives.

Think of how far you've come, of how many changes since that first prayer, "Out of the depths" to this stirring affirmation: "I shall not die, but live."

To have forged a new relationship with yourself and, with God's help then move on to address the errors of your past, this indeed is grace.

I will lift up mine eyes unto the hills, from whence cometh my help. My help cometh from the Lord, which made Heaven and earth. He will not suffer thy foot to be moved: he that keepeth thee will not slumber. Behold, he that keepeth Israel shall neither slumber nor sleep. The Lord is thy keeper: the Lord is thy shade upon thy right hand. The sun shall not smite thee by day, nor the moon by night. The Lord shall preserve thee from all evil: he shall preserve thy soul. The Lord shall preserve thy going out and thy coming in from this time forth, and even for evermore.

PSALM 121

Our God, we desire to bless and praise thee for thy unspeakable mercy for restoring him who was sick to health. In the time of sickness thou wast indeed gracious unto us. Thy chastening hand was upon us, but it was a hand of love. Grant that this visitation may never be forgotten by us. May it have left many a blessing behind it. May our future life be marked by more devotedness to our Savior, more humility, more love, more earnestness of heart and life. O Holy Spirit, deepen thy·work in our souls. Sanctify us wholly, so that we may be more entirely thine than we have ever been before. Take up thine abode with us. Comfort us with thine indwelling Presence. May we live henceforth only to thy glory.

BISHOP ASHTON OXENDEN

❧

Give us, O Lord, a humble spirit, that we may never
presume upon thy mercy, but live always as those who
have been much forgiven. Make us tender and
compassionate toward any who are overtaken by
temptation, remembering how we have fallen in times
past and may fall yet again. Make us watchful and
sober-minded, looking ever unto thee for grace to stand
upright, and to persevere unto the end.

CHARLES J. VAUGHAN

❧

How often, almighty God, when we are wavering and
helpless, uncertain and troubled in thought, and unwise
in conduct, do we look around for a guide of
unquestioned authority, who by his eminence has
distanced all competition and silenced all envy, and who
may lead us through the mazes of life! But are we always
prompted by a genuine feeling of humility? Is it not too
often vanity or pride that misleads us? Are we conscious
of our own feebleness and our own shortcomings? Is our
self-respect really so low, or is not our estimation of our
brethren too small and slender? If we could think more
highly of our neighbors, and banish self-conceit, how
often might we not be strengthened by advice, concord,
and unity, and go forth with our fellow-pilgrims, not like
the devastating locusts, but laboring diligently and
anxiously, and thus cause prosperity and happiness to
prevail around us! Incline our hearts, almighty God, to
love and serve one another; so shall we be stronger and
more powerful for all good actions, for all deeds of
usefulness, than if we merely look for assistance to the

few, who, by the grace of thy Providence, our heavenly
Father, may have been placed in a higher sphere of
intellectual distinction or worldly greatness!

ANONYMOUS

O holy and most gracious Master and Savior Jesus, who
by thy example and by thy precept, by the practice of a
whole life and frequent discourses, didst command us to
be meek and humble, in imitation of thy incomparable
sweetness and great humility, be pleased to give me the
grace, as thou hast given me the commandment: enable
me to do whatsoever thou commandest, and command
whatsoever thou pleasest.

O mortify in me all proud thoughts and vain
opinions of myself; let me return to thee the
acknowledgment and the fruits of all those good things
thou hast given me, that, by confessing I am wholly in
debt to thee for them, I may not boast myself for what I
have received, and for what I am highly accountable; and
for what is my own teach me to be ashamed and
humbled, it being nothing but sin and misery, weakness
and uncleanness.

Let me go before my brethren in nothing but
striving to do them honor and thee glory, never to seek
my own praise, never to delight in it when it is offered;
that, despising myself, I may be accepted by thee in the
honors with which thou shalt crown thy humble and
despised servants, for Jesus' sake, in the kingdom of
eternal glory.

JEREMY TAYLOR

79

❧

Make us, O Lord, to be humble without feigning, true
without duplicity, afraid of thee without despair, hopeful
without presumption, loving without dissimulation, and
patient without murmuring. Bestow on us intelligence to
know thee, diligence to seek thee, wisdom to find thee, a
conversation pleasing unto thee, and perseverance to
expect thee confidently, through Jesus Christ our Lord.

SAINT THOMAS AQUINAS

❧

Of all the days of the year, which thy divine bounty,
Lord God Almighty, allows us to pass on earth, not one
is more solemn than this; it brings the past vividly and
powerfully before us, and, with it, our blemishes, our
shortcomings, and the faults that have led us into error
and misery, and that may have caused sadness and grief
to others, or bereft us of the strength of serving them.
What atonement can we make, alas! for our weakness,
for having wavered and failed in the fulfillment of duty,
drifted into infirmity of purpose, mental lassitude, and
moral listlessness, for having been idle and neglectful in
the work of self-improvement, for having abandoned
labors of usefulness, and allowed rank weeds to luxuriate
in heart and mind, which should teem with every flower
of sweetness, every generous fruit of charity, and with all
good harvests of thought and deed? O God of mercy and
of omnipotence, we are truly helpless without thy divine
aid; forgive us and assist us that we may keep aloof from
sin, and learn to live well and usefully in accordance
with thy holy will, and thus earn and merit the precious
blessing of life!

JEWISH ATONEMENT PRAYER

Wilt thou forgive that sinne where I begunne,
Which is my sin, though it were done before?
Wilt thou forgive those sinnes, through which I
    runne,
And do run still: though still I do deplore?
When thou hast done, thou hast not done,
For, I have more.

    Wilt thou forgive that sinne by which I'have
  wonne
Others to sinne? and, made my sinne their doore?
Wilt thou forgive that sinne which I did shunne
A yeare, or two: but wallowed in, a score?
When thou hast done, thou hast not done,
For, I have more.

    I have a sinne of feare, that when I have
  spunne
My last thred, I shall perish on the shore;
Sweare by thy selfe, that at my death thy sonne
Shall shine as he shines now, and heretofore;
And, having done that, thou haste done,
I feare no more.

                                        JOHN DONNE

Lord, make me an instrument of thy peace. Where there
is hatred, let me sow love; where there is injury, pardon;
where there is doubt, faith; where there is despair, hope;
where there is darkness, light; where there is sadness, joy.
    O Divine Master, grant that I may not so much
seek to be consoled, as to console; to be understood, as to

understand; to be loved, as to love. For it is in giving that we receive, it is in pardoning that we are pardoned; it is in dying that we are born to eternal life.

SAINT FRANCIS OF ASSISI

O thou who coverest thyself with light as with a garment, shine thou in us, putting to flight all the forces of darkness and guilt, of sin and selfishness. Shine also through us to any that live in shadow, and so fill us with thy radiant spirit that we may be a lamp unto a neighbor's feet and a light unto his path. And when this day is done, may every face we have met be the brighter for our meeting, and every heart braver, with new joy and cheer and grace and strength.

THEODORE PARKER

Our Father, we acknowledge our manifold sins—we do earnestly repent and are heartily sorry for these our misdoings. We have done those things we ought not to have done and we have left undone those things we ought to have done. Have mercy upon us, O God, and teach us to have mercy on ourselves by learning never to follow a first mistake by a second—always to learn the future by the past, and ever to rise on stepping-stones of our dead selves to higher things. Amen.

W. E. B. DuBOIS

To yield is to be preserved whole.
To be bent is to become straight.
To be hollow is to be filled.

To be tattered is to be renewed.
To be in want is to possess.
To have plenty is to be confused.

Therefore the Sage embraces the One,
And becomes the model of the world.
He does not reveal himself,
And is therefore luminous.
He does not justify himself,
And is therefore far-famed.
He does not boast of himself,
And therefore people give him credit.
He does not pride himself,
And is therefore the ruler among men.

It is because he does not contend
That no one in the world can contend against him.

Is it not indeed true, as the ancients say,
"To yield is to be preserved whole"?
Thus he is preserved and the world does him
homage.

LAO TZU

8

· · · : · · · · · · · · · · · · · · · · ·

Even the Sparrow
Finds a Home

Having established a relationship with God, and having begun to forge a new identity with God's help, it is time to reach out to others.

If we have closed accounts on the emotional blackmail we have done to ourselves, it is now time to close our accounts with others. By taking stock of ourselves in our relationship with others, and by changing our attitudes and behavior lovingly and without expectation, we can free ourselves from traps we set in our past.

By defining whom we've hurt, we see who we have been. By becoming willing to change, we confirm who we have become.

❧

How lovely is thy dwelling place, O Lord of hosts! My
soul longs, yea, faints for the courts of the Lord; my
heart and flesh sing for joy to the living God. Even the
sparrow finds a home, and the swallow a nest for herself,
where she may lay her young, at thy altars, O Lord of
hosts, my King and my God. Blessed are those who
dwell in thy house, ever singing thy praise! Blessed are
the men whose strength is in thee, in whose heart are the
highways to Zion. As they go through the valley of Baca
they make it a place of springs; the early rain also covers
it with pools. They go from strength to strength; the
God of gods will be seen in Zion. O Lord God of hosts,
hear my prayer; give ear, O God of Jacob! Behold our
shield, O God; look upon the face of thine anointed! For
a day in thy courts is better than a thousand elsewhere. I
would rather be a doorkeeper in the house of my God
than dwell in the tents of wickedness. For the Lord God
is a sun and shield; he bestows favor and honor. No
good thing does the Lord withhold from those who walk
uprightly. O Lord of hosts, blessed is the man who trusts
in thee!

PSALM 84

❧

O Lord God, almighty and all-merciful,
Cleanse those whom I have defiled,
Heal those whom I have wounded,

Strengthen those whom I have enfeebled,
Set right those whom I have misled,
Recall to thyself those whom I have alienated from
   thee.
I pray thee, save these sinners.
Save all sinners,
And amongst all sinners save me the sinner,
For Jesus' sake, the Friend of sinners.

ANONYMOUS

God, be patient with me, and make those who love me
patient. Forgive, and help them to forgive, my weak
resolve, my stubborn pride. Father, I know how I hurt
thee, and them, when I am unreasonable and demanding,
when I lose my temper over trivial things. Make me
stronger, O God; help me to keep the promises I make at
night to thee and to them to mend my ways on the
morrow. Help me to be patient and forgiving with them
as thou art and they are with me. When I am in the
wrong give me the grace to admit it wholly, neither
offering excuses nor trying to shift the blame. Make me
more honest in my thinking, more charitable in my
opinions. Father, in thy mercy thou hast given me the
love of family and friends; in thy mercy help me to be
worthy of it.

ANONYMOUS

Almighty and everlasting God, from whom and through
whom and in whom all things are, from whose hand we,
with all the world besides, every moment take our being:
We appear before thee humbly to acknowledge that thou

art the one true God, boundless in thy power, wisdom, goodness, the maker of all things made, the watchful witness and just judge of all things done.

Have mercy, O Lord, have mercy on us sinners. We repent of our sins, we wish they were undone; they cannot be undone, but thou canst pardon them. We humbly hope to be forgiven.

Help us for thy sake to love our neighbors, all men, wishing them well, not ill; proposing to do them good, not evil; forgiving also all who have offended us, as we by thee hope to be forgiven.

GERARD MANLEY HOPKINS

May I be no man's enemy, and may I be the friend of that which is eternal and abides. May I never quarrel with those nearest me; and if I do, may I be reconciled quickly. May I never devise evil against any man; if any devise evil against me, may I escape uninjured and without the need of hurting him. May I love, seek, and attain only that which is good. May I wish for all men's happiness and envy none. May I never rejoice in the ill fortune of one who has wronged me. When I have done or said what is wrong, may I never wait for the rebuke of others, but always rebuke myself until I make amends. . . . May I win no victory that harms either me or my opponent. . . . May I reconcile friends who are wroth with one another. May I, to the extent of my power, give all needful help to my friends and to all who are in want. May I never fail a friend in danger. When visiting those in grief may I be able by gentle and healing words to soften their pain. . . . May I respect myself. . . . May I always keep tame that which rages within me. . . . May I accustom myself to be gentle, and never be angry with

people because of circumstances. May I never discuss
who is wicked and what wicked things he has done, but
know good men and follow in their footsteps.

EUSEBIUS OF CAESAREA

I offer up unto thee my prayers and intercessions, for
those especially who have in any matter hurt or grieved
me or found fault with me or who have done me any
damage or displeasure—

For those also whom, at any time, I may have vexed
and troubled by words or deeds, knowingly or in
ignorance; that thou wouldst grant us all equally pardon
for our sins and for our offenses against each other—

Take away from our hearts, O Lord, all
suspiciousness, indignation, wrath, and contention, and
whatsoever may hurt charity and lessen brotherly love.
Have mercy, O Lord, have mercy on those that crave
thy mercy, give grace unto them that stand in need
thereof, and make us such as that we may be worthy to
enjoy thy grace and go forward to life eternal.

THOMAS À KEMPIS

Forgive me O Lord, O Lord forgive me my sinnes, the
sinnes of my youth, and my present sinnes, the sinne
that my parents cast upon me, originall sinne, and the
sinnes that I cast upon my children, in an ill example;
actuall sinnes, sinnes which are manifest to all the world,
and sinnes which I have so labored to hide from the
world, as that now they are hid from mine own
conscience, and mine own memory; forgive me my
crying sins, and my whispering sins, sins of uncharitable

hate, and sinnes of unchaste love, sinnes against thee and thee, against thy power, O almighty Father, against thy wisedome, O glorious Sonne, against thy goodnesse, O blessed Spirit of God; and sinnes against him and him, against superiors and equals, and inferiors; and sinnes against me and me, against mine own soul, and against my body, which I have loved better than my soul; forgive me O Lord, O Lord in the merits of thy Christ and my Jesus, thine Anointed, and my Savior; forgive me my sinnes, all my sinnes.

JOHN DONNE

Give me, O Lord, a mild, a peaceable, a meek, and a humble spirit, that, remembering my own infirmities, I may bear with those of others; that, considering my character, I may rebuke with all long-suffering and gravity; that I may think lowly of myself, and not be angry when others also think lowly of me; that I may be patient toward all men, gentle and easy to be entreated, that God, for Christ's sake, may be so toward me.

BISHOP WILSON

O God, preserve me from evil allurements and keep me from all tribulations. Make good both my inward and my outward man and cleanse my heart from hatred and envy. Let not any man have any issue against me.

O God, I seek of thee to lay hold of the good and to forsake the evil, as thou knowest them. Undertake, I pray thee, for my protection and give me simplicity in my living and by clear guidance a way out of all dubiety and victory with the right in every argument.

Grant me to be just, both in anger and in good pleasure, and submissive to what the decree brings. Make me moderate both in poverty and wealth, humble in word and deed, and truthful in jest and earnest.

O God, I have trespassed in my relationship with thee, and I have trespassed in my relationship to thy creation. O God, forgive my trespasses against thee and bear off from me my trespasses against thy creation. Enrich me with thy goodness. For thou art plenteous in forgiveness.

O God, enlighten my heart with knowledge and employ my body in thy obedience. Save me from the machinations of my heart and occupy my thoughts with thy esteem.

PRAYERS OF THE NAQSHABANDI ORDER

Most merciful and loving Father,
We beseech thee most humbly, even with all our
    hearts,
To pour out upon our enemies with bountiful
    hands whatsoever things thou knowest may do
    them good.
And chiefly a sound and uncorrupt mind,
Where-through they may know thee and love thee
    in true charity and with their whole heart.
And love us, thy children, for thy sake.
Let not their first hating of us turn to their harm,
Seeing that we cannot do them good for want of
    ability.
Lord, we desire their amendment and our own.
Separate them not from us by punishing them,
But join and knot them to us by thy favorable
    dealing with them.

And, seeing we be all ordained to be citizens of the
    one everlasting city,
Let us begin to enter into that way here already by
    mutual love,
Which may bring us right forth thither.

ELIZABETHAN PRAYER

Lord, our God, great, eternal, wonderful in glory, who
keepest covenant and promise for those that love thee
with their whole heart; who art the Life of all, the Help
of those that flee unto thee, the Hope of those who cry
unto thee; cleanse us from our sins, secret and open, and
from every thought displeasing to thy goodness; cleanse
our bodies and souls, our hearts and consciences, that
with a pure heart and a clear soul, with perfect love and
calm hope, we may venture confidently and fearlessly to
pray unto thee.

COPTIC LITURGY OF SAINT BASIL

Give us, O Lord, a mind after thine own heart, that we
may delight to do thy will, O Lord; and let thy law be
written in our hearts. Give us courage and resolution to
do our duty, and a heart to be spent in thy service and
in doing all the good that possibly we can the few
remaining days of our pilgrimage here on earth.

ARCHBISHOP JOHN TILLOTSON

93

9

·················

How Good
and Pleasant It Is

Some relationships need restoration, some revision, some renewal. As we venture back to old hurts and make amends, we engage in a twofold process. At first, we see the changes in ourselves as we are no longer subject to the guilt that has held us in thrall.

We can now walk down the street fearlessly, openly. And, to some extent, recognition of patterns in our past relationships allows us to change the way we form future relationships.

We have been able to come to completeness and integration with ourselves, others, and God. We have become "a part of," rather than "apart from." And we have participated in and have become reflections of the creative process of divinity itself: order from chaos, liberation from bondage, love from fear.

Martin Luther King called it the "Strength to Love."

❧

Behold, how good and pleasant it is when brothers dwell
in unity! It is like the precious oil upon the head,
running down upon the beard, upon the beard of Aaron,
running down on the collar of his robes! It is like the
dew of Hermon, which falls on the mountains of Zion!
For there the Lord has commanded the blessing, life for
evermore.

PSALM 133

❧

Grant, Lord, that we might overcome our enemies by
transforming them into friends. Make them and make us
conscious of those deep inward reaches whereby every
heart is rooted in our world's deep common life. Cause
us to cease looking into the directions that oppose. Cause
us, O thou our Utmost Good, to look into the one
direction of a united look unto thee.

JEWISH PRAYER

❧

O God our Father, good beyond all that is good, fair
beyond all that is fair, in whom is calmness, peace, and
concord; do thou make up the dissensions which divide
us from each other, and bring us back into a unity of
love, which may bear some likeness to thy sublime
Nature. And as thou art above all things, so we pray

thee, that through the embrace of charity and the bonds
of affection we may be spiritually one, as well in
ourselves as in each other, through that peace of thine
which maketh all things peaceful, and through the grace,
mercy, and tenderness of thine only-begotten Son.

SYRIAN CLEMENTINE LITURGY

Give us, O God, the gift of human charity. Lead us to
know that bad as human nature is and black as our
passion may be, that most men are always a little better
than the worst, always more decent than our rash
judgment tries to paint. Give us the humility to realize
that few of us put in their places—with their hurts and
hindrances and their vision of right—few of us would do
better than they, and many would do far worse. Perhaps
God meant just this when he said: Blessed are the meek.

W. E. B. DuBois

Almighty and most merciful God, we beseech thee to
give us grace to love thee with all our hearts, and our
neighbor as ourselves. Endue us with charitable and
upright dispositions, and with humble and contented
minds in every condition of life. Conduct us continually
to higher degrees of wisdom and excellence. Purify us
from all vicious habits and passions. Dispose us heartily
to every good work, that we may be proper objects of
thy favor and blessing.

UNITARIAN PRAYER

O giver of thyself! at the vision of thee as joy let our souls flame up to thee as the fire, flow on to thee as the river, permeate thy being as the fragrance of the flower. Give us strength to love, to love fully, our life in its joys and sorrows, in its gains and losses, in its rise and fall. Let us have strength enough fully to see and hear thy universe and to work with full vigor therein. Let us fully live the life thou hast given us, let us bravely take and bravely give. This is our prayer to thee. Let us once for all dislodge from our minds the feeble fancy that would make out thy joy to be a thing apart from action, thin, formless, and unsustained. Wherever the peasant tills the hard earth, there does thy joy gush out in the green of the corn, wherever man displaces the entangled forest, smooths the stony ground, and clears for himself a homestead, there does thy joy enfold it in orderliness and peace.

O worker of the universe! We would pray to thee to let the irresistible current of thy universal energy come like the impetuous south wind of spring, let it come rushing over the vast field of the life of man, let it bring the scent of many flowers, the murmurings of many woodlands, let it make sweet and vocal the lifelessness of our dried-up soul-life. Let our newly awakened powers cry out for unlimited fulfillment in leaf and flower and fruit.

RABINDRANATH TAGORE

O God, whose fatherly care reacheth to the uttermost parts of the earth: We humbly beseech thee graciously to behold and bless those whom we love, now absent from

99

us. Defend them from all dangers of soul and body; and
grant that both they and we, drawing nearer to thee,
may be bound together by thy love in the communion of
thy Holy Spirit, and in the fellowship of thy saints,
through Jesus Christ our Lord.

BOOK OF COMMON PRAYER

May I never cause pain to any living being.
May I never utter untruth, and
May I never covet the wealth or wife of another.
May I ever drink the nectar of contentment.
May I always entertain a feeling of friendliness for
    all living beings in the world.
May the spring of sympathy in my heart be ever
    bubbling to those in agony and affliction.
May I never feel angry with the vile, the vicious,
    and the wrongly directed.
May there be an adjustment of things that I shall
    always remain tranquil in dealing with them.

Whether people speak of me well or ill
Whether wealth comes to me or departs
Whether I live to be hundreds of thousands of years
    old or give up the spirit this day
Whether anyone holds out any kind of fears
Or with worldly riches he tempts me
In the face of all these possible things
May my footsteps swerve not from the path of
    truth.

With pleasure may the mind not be puffed up
Let pain disturb it never
May the awesome loneliness of a mountain, forest,
   or river
Or a burning place, never cause it to shiver,
Unmoved, unshakeable, in firmness may it grow
   adamantine
And display true moral strength when parted from
   the desired thing,
Or united with the undesired.
May there be mutual love in the world.
May delusion dwell at a distance
May no one ever utter unpleasant speech
Or words that are harsh lies ensue.
May all understand the Laws of Truth
   and joyfully sorrow and sufferings endure
Om, peace, Shanti, Shanti, Shanti.

JAIN PRAYER

O God, Father of all, help us to forgive others as we
would wish them to forgive us. May we try to
understand them as we in turn would like to be
understood, in the hope that forgiveness will not be in
order. May we see with their eyes, think with their
minds, feel with their hearts. Then let us ask ourselves
whether we should judge them, or judge ourselves and
accept them as children, like us, of one heavenly Father.

WILLIAM BARCLAY

Almighty God, our heavenly Father, who lovest all and
forgettest none, we bring to thee our supplications for all
thy creatures and all thy children.

For all whom we love and for whom we watch and care:
We beseech thee to hear us.

For all who have blessed us with kindness, led us
with patience, restored us with their sympathy and help,
and whose charity has covered a multitude of our sins:
We beseech thee.

For all who have wished or done us ill, that thou
wouldst turn their hearts to penitence and ours to
blessing:
We beseech thee.

For all dumb creatures; that men may be merciful,
and touched with a feeling of their infirmities:
We beseech thee to hear us.

For all prisoners and captives, and all suffering from
oppression, that thou wilt manifest thy mercy toward
them, and make the heart of man merciful as thine own:
We beseech thee.

For all on whom thou hast laid the cross of
suffering, the sick in body and the feeble in mind; for all
who are in danger, necessity, and tribulation; and all who
travel by land or by water:
We beseech thee.

For all who have been bereaved of relatives and
friends, or are troubled by the suffering or sin of those
they love:
We beseech thee to hear us.

For all who are visited by worldly loss, that in the
dark and cloudy day they may find the peace of God:
We beseech thee to hear us.

For all who are absorbed in their own grief, that
they may be raised to share the sorrows of their brethren,
and know the secret and blessed fellowship of the Cross:
We beseech thee.

For all who do justly, love mercy, and walk humbly
with God, that grace and peace may rest upon them:

We beseech thee.

For all who are suffering because of their
faithfulness to conviction and duty, that renunciation
may bring strength, and sacrifice hope, and that they
may have the grace, who seest in secret, and come at last
to an open reward:

We beseech thee to hear us, O God.

For all perplexed by the deeper questions of life,
overshadowed with doubt, and concerned lest even in
thought they should depart from thee, that light may
arise in their darkness:

We beseech thee to hear us.

For the careless, the scornful, the lovers of darkness
rather than light, that they may be delivered from the
bonds of iniquity:

We beseech thee.

For all who are tried by passionate temptations, or
cold ambitions, or mean suggestions, that thy mercy may
be their salvation:

We beseech thee to hear us, O God.

For all who are lonely and sad in the midst of
others' joys, that they may know God as their Friend
and Comforter:

We beseech thee.

For the infirm and aged, and all who are growing
weary with the journey of life; and for all who are
passing through the valley of death; that they may find
comfort and strength in God, and light at evening time:

We beseech thee to hear us.

For all forgotten by us, but dear to thee:

We beseech thee to hear us, O God.

O God our Father, have regard to our intercessions,
answer them according to thy will, and make us the
channels of thine infinite pity and helpfulness.

JOHN HUNTER

O God, may our souls be warm with life. Save us from
an inanimate and sluggish state. Teach us thy purity;
how great thy abhorrence of evil, how irreconcilable thy
hatred of it; and may we all partake of the same
abhorrence of sin.

Increase our sensibility to evil; may we shun every
appearance of it, and repel the first temptation; and, in a
world where example is so corrupt, we beseech thee to
arm us with a holy fortitude.

Inspire us with a generous love of virtue, of
rectitude, of holiness. May we prefer it even to life.
Animate us to adhere to good in every danger. May
nothing on earth move us or shake our steadfastness.
Increase our sensibility to good; may we see more and
more its loveliness and beauty.

Animate us to cheerfulness. May we have a joyful
sense of our blessings, learn to look on the bright
circumstances of our lot, and maintain a perpetual
contentedness under thy allotments.

Fortify our minds against disappointment and
calamity. Preserve us from despondency, from yielding
to dejection. Teach us that no evil is intolerable but a
guilty conscience; and that nothing can hurt us, if with
true loyalty of affection we keep thy commandments and
take refuge in thee.

May every day add brightness and energy to our
conceptions of thy lovely and glorious character. Give us
a deeper sense of thy presence, and instruct us to nourish
our devoutness by every scene of nature and every event
of Providence.

Assist us to consecrate our whole being and
existence to thee, our understandings to the knowledge
of thy character, our hearts to the veneration and love of

thy perfections, our wills to the choice of thy commands,
our active energies to the accomplishment of thy
purposes, our lives to thy glory, and every power to the
imitation of thy goodness. Be thou the center, life, and
sovereign of our souls!

WILLIAM ELLERY CHANNING

Almighty and eternal God, who hast sent us into this
world to live according to thy laws, look in mercy upon
us, we beseech thee; and enable us to do our duty wisely
hour by hour. Grant that having served our generation,
we may be gathered to our fathers with the comfort of a
reasonable hope in thee, and in perfect charity with all
men; so that neither life nor death, nor principalities nor
powers, nor things present nor things to come, nor
height nor depth, nor any other creature may be able to
separate us from the love of God.

JEREMY TAYLOR

10

....

This Is the Day

"This is the day which the Lord hath made; we will rejoice and be glad in it" (Psalm 118).

Everything deteriorates without proper maintenance. Cars, houses, paperwork—all demand attention and upkeep. If you haven't used a foreign language in a while, you can't assume that you remember it. You may even have forgotten the basic grammar. That's what sobriety is like, strong yet fragile, requiring daily commitment to maintain and preserve.

Daily examination allows us to assess our relationships and growth, to continue the process of humility, of joining with others.

All great saints and sages knew the secret of spiritual life—that it is daily. Horace Bushnell spoke of "living to God in small things." Tapestries are stitched. Live . . . to God . . . in . . . small . . . things.

❧

Hear my cry, O God, listen to my prayer; from the end
of the earth I call to thee, when my heart is faint. Lead
thou me to the rock that is higher than I; for thou art
my refuge, a strong tower against the enemy. Let me
dwell in thy tent forever! Oh to be safe under the shelter
of thy wings! For thou, O God, hast heard my vows,
thou hast given me the heritage of those who fear thy
name. . . . So will I ever sing praises to thy name, as I
pay my vows day after day.

PSALM 61

❧

We beseech thee, O our God, that we may know thee,
love thee, and rejoice in thee; and if in this life we
cannot do these things fully, grant that we may progress
in them from day to day. Advance in us a true
knowledge of thee now, that in the life to come it may
be complete: increase in us the love of thee here, that
there it may be full, through Jesus Christ our Lord.

SAINT ANSELM

❧

O God, as the day returns and brings us the petty round
of irritating duties, help us to perform them with
laughter and kind faces; let cheerfulness abound with

industry. Give us to go blithely on our business all this day, bring us to our resting beds weary and content and undishonored, and grant us in the end the gift of sleep.

ROBERT LEWIS STEVENSON

❧

O Lord, our heavenly Father, without whom all purposes are frustrate, all efforts are vain, grant us the assistance of the Holy Spirit, that we may not sorrow as those without hope, but may now return to the duties of our present life with humble confidence in thy protection, and so govern our thoughts and actions that no business or work may ever withdraw our minds from thee, but that in the changes of this life we may fix our hearts upon the reward which thou hast promised to them that serve thee, and that whatever things are true, whatever things are honest, whatever things are just, whatever things are pure, whatever things are lovely, whatever things are of good report, wherein there is virtue, wherein there is praise, we may think upon and do, and obtain mercy, consolation, and everlasting happiness.

SAMUEL JOHNSON

❧

Let me but do my work from day to day,
In field or forest, at the desk or loom,
In roaring marketplace or tranquil room;
Let me but find it in my heart to say,
When vagrant wishes beckon me astray,
"This is my work; my blessing, not my doom;
Of all who live, I am the one by whom
This work can best be done in the right way."

Then shall I see it not too great, nor small,
To suit my spirit and to prove my powers;
Then shall I cheerful greet the laboring hours,
And cheerful turn, when the long shadows fall
At eventide, to play and love and rest,
Because I know for me my work is best.

HENRY VAN DYKE

O Lord who, in infinite wisdom and love, orderest all
things for thy children, order everything this day for me
in thy tender pity. Thou knowest my weakness; thou
knowest how my soul shrinks from all pain of soul. Lord
I know that thou wilt lay no greater burden on me than
thou canst help me to bear. Teach me to receive all
things this day from thee. Enable me to commend myself
in all things to thee. Grant me in all things to please
thee; bring me through all things nearer unto thee; bring
me, day by day, nearer to thyself, to life everlasting.

Teach me, O Father, how to ask thee each moment,
silently, for thy help. If I am disquieted, enable me, by
thy grace, to turn to thee. May nothing this day come
between me and thee. Work thy holy will in me and
through me. Guide me, bless me, that I may do
something this day for love of thee, that I may this
evening be nearer to thee though I know it not. Lead
me, O Lord, in a straight way unto thyself, and keep me
in thy grace unto the end.

E. B. PUSEY

O God, who knowest and accomplishest what is best, be
it unto us according to thy will. For this we know that
thou desirest to deliver us from evil.

III

From every fault, known and unknown,
Good Lord! deliver us.
From self-indulgence and fretfulness, from loss of
temper and waste of time,
Good Lord! deliver us.
From indecision and haste, from vacillation and all
day-dreaming,
Good Lord! deliver us.
From perplexity and rashness, from impatience and
discontent,
Good Lord! deliver us.
From pride and arrogance, from self-sufficiency and
all distrust of thee,
Good Lord! deliver us.
Spirit of truth and of light, shine into our hearts,
we pray thee, now and at all times; illumine our minds
with the knowledge of thyself, and guide us in the right
way; that so we may walk undismayed through all the
perplexities of this world; doing our daily work in all
modesty, simplicity, and patience; bearing our burdens,
because they are thy will; and persevering in the practice
of all the virtues of thy children, whom thou hast called
unto fellowship with thyself, through Jesus Christ our
Lord.

BOOK OF COMMON PRAYER

❧

Lord, teach me to serve thee as thou deservest . . .
To give, and not to count the cost
To fight, and not to heed the wounds
To labor, and not to ask for rest save knowing that
I do thy will.

SAINT IGNATIUS LOYOLA

꒰

Grant me, even me, my dearest Lord, to know thee, and
love thee, and rejoice in thee. If I cannot do these
perfectly in this life, let me at least advance to higher
degrees every day, till I can come to do them in
perfection. Let the knowledge of thee increase in me
here, that it may be full hereafter. Let the love of thee
grow every day more and more here, that it may be
perfect hereafter; that my joy may be great in itself, and
full in thee. I know, O God, that thou art a God of
truth; O make good thy gracious promises to me, that
my joy may be full.

SAINT AUGUSTINE

꒰

O merciful God! Eternal Light shining in darkness.
Thou who dispellest the night of sin and all blindness of
heart, since thou hast appointed the night for rest and
the day for labor, we beseech thee grant that our bodies
may rest in peace and quietness, that afterward they may
be able to endure the labor they must bear. Temper our
sleep that it be not disorderly, that we may remain
spotless both in body and soul, yea that even our sleep
itself may be to thy glory. Enlighten the eyes of our
understanding that we may not sleep in death but always
look for deliverance from this misery. Defend us against
all assaults of the Devil and take us into thy holy
protection. And although we have not passed this day
without greatly sinning against thee, we beseech thee to
hide our sins with thy mercy as thou hidest all things on

earth with the darkness of the night, that we may not be cast out from thy presence. Relieve and comfort all those who are afflicted in mind, body, or estate.

JOHN CALVIN

This day is mine to mar or make,
God keep me strong and true;
Let me no erring bypath take,
No doubtful action do.

Grant me, when with the setting sun
This fleeting day shall end,
I may rejoice o'er something done,
Be richer by a friend.

Let all I meet along the way
Speak well of me tonight,
I would not have the humblest say
I'd hurt him by a slight.

Let me be patient and serene,
Gentle and kind and fair,
Help me to keep my record clean
Through all that I must bear.

Grant that because I live today,
And to my thoughts give voice,
O'er something he shall hear me say
Another shall rejoice.

Let there be something true and fine
When night slips down, to tell
That I have lived this day of mine
Not selfishly, but well.

EDGAR A. GUEST

The sun has disappeared.
I have switched off the light,
and my wife and children are asleep.
The animals in the forest are full of fear,
and so are the people on their mats.
They prefer the day with your sun
to the night.
But I still know that
your moon is there,
and your eyes
and also your hands.
Thus I am not afraid.
This day again
you led us wonderfully.
Everybody went to his mat
satisfied and full.
Renew us during our sleep,
that in the morning
we may come afresh to our daily jobs.
Be with our brothers far away in Asia
who may be getting up now.
Amen.

AFRICAN PRAYER

11

....

Thou Preservest Me from Trouble

Spiritual exercise is like physical and intellectual exercise. It avails us little unless we practice it regularly.

The Gospel of Matthew assures us: "Seek and you shall find." We seek God's will for us because the evidence is that when we do so, our lives and the lives of those with whom we come into contact become better.

Carl Jung thought that recovery from addictive illness was possible only if there was a radical transformation of the personality based on spiritual principles. Our relationship with God has now become conscious—a deep, adult, ongoing relationship that will continue to deepen and broaden as we wake up to the miracle not only of being free of our addiction, but also of having achieved that freedom.

※

Blessed is he whose transgression is forgiven, whose sin is covered. Blessed is the man to whom the Lord imputes no iniquity, and in whose spirit there is no deceit. When I declared not my sin, my body wasted away through my groaning all day long. For day and night thy hand was heavy upon me; my strength was dried up as by the heat of summer. I acknowledged my sin to thee, and I did not hide my iniquity; I said, "I will confess my transgressions to the Lord"; then thou didst forgive the guilt of my sin. Therefore let every one who is godly offer prayer to thee; at a time of distress, in the rush of great waters, they shall not reach him. Thou art a hiding place for me, thou preservest me from trouble; thou dost encompass me with deliverance. I will instruct you and teach you the way you should go; I will counsel you with my eye upon you. Be not like a horse or a mule, without understanding, which must be curbed with bit and bridle, else it will not keep with you. Many are the pangs of the wicked; but steadfast love surrounds him who trusts in the Lord. Be glad in the Lord, and rejoice, O righteous, and shout for joy, all you upright in heart!

PSALM 32

※

O Thou eternal Lord God, in whose appointment our life standeth, thou hast committed to us our work, and we would commit to thee our cares. May we wait upon

thy seasons, and leave ourselves to thee. May we feel that
we are not our own; and that thou wilt heed our wants
whilst we are intent upon thy will. May we never walk
anxiously, as if our path were hid, but with a mind fixed
simply upon the charge entrusted to us, and desiring
nothing but the dispositions of thy providence. More and
more fill us with a pity for others' trouble, which shall
bring forgetfulness of our own; with the charity of them
that know their own unworthiness; with the promptitude
of them that dare not boast of tomorrow; and with the
glad hope of the children of eternity. Lead us in the
straight path of simplicity and sanctity; and let neither
the flatteries nor the censures of men draw us aside from
it. And unto thee, the Beginning and the End, Lord of
the living and Refuge of the dying, be thanks and praise
forever.

JAMES MARTINEAU

O most gracious Lord, the God of the spirits of all flesh,
in whose hand my time is, I praise and magnify thee,
that thou hast in love to my soul delivered me from the
pit of destruction, and restored me to health again. It is
of thy mercy alone, O Lord, that thou hast preserved my
life from destruction; thou hast chastened and corrected
me, but thou hast not given me over unto death. O let
this life which thou hast thus graciously spared be
wholly consecrated unto thee. Behold, O Lord, I am by
thy mercy made whole. . . . Let not this reprieve thou
hast now given me make me secure, as thinking my
Lord delayeth his coming; but grant me, I beseech thee,
to make a right use of this long-suffering of thine, and so
employ every minute of that time thou hast allowed me,

that when thou shalt appear, I may have confidence, and not be ashamed before thee at thy coming.

Lord, I have found by this approach toward death how dreadful a thing it is to be taken unprepared. O let it be a perpetual admonition to me to watch for my Master's coming; and when the pleasures of sin shall present themselves to entice me, O make me to remember how bitter they will be at the last. O Lord, hear me, and as thou hast in much mercy afforded me time, so grant me all grace to work out my salvation, to provide oil in my lamp, that when the Bridegroom cometh, I may go in with him to the marriage; grant this I beseech thee, for thy dear Son's sake.

SCALA SANCTA

O Lord, Creator,
Ruler of the world, Father,
I thank, thank, thank you
that you have brought me through.
How strong the pain was—
but you were stronger.
How deep the fall was—
but you were even deeper.
How dark was the night—
but you were the noonday sun in it.
You are our father,
our mother,
our brother, and our friend.
Your grace has no end,
and your light no snuffer.
We praise you,
we honor you,

and we pray to your holy name.
We thank you
that you rule thus,
and that you are so merciful
with your tired followers.

AFRICAN PRAYER

Some things there are I must not do:
To self I must not be untrue,
I must not for a profit's sake
A false or mean advantage take,
Or risk an everlasting stain
For selfish pride or paltry gain.

I must not thoughtlessly deride
The things which are my neighbor's pride,
Or hold my head so high that he
May fear to make a friend of me.
I must not, though it be my right,
Disturb his comfort, day or night.

I must not disregard life's laws,
Or think myself secure because
The vile may prosper and the cheat
May seem to flourish in deceit.
If happiness I hope to reap,
Both health and honor I must keep.

Lord, when temptation comes along,
'Tis then, I pray thee, make me strong.
Let neither fame, nor wealth, nor prize,
To what is manly blind my eyes.

Let it be said, when life is through,
Some things there were I would not do.

EDGAR A. GUEST

❧

O beloved Pan and all ye other gods of this place, grant
to me that I be made beautiful in my soul within, and
that all external possessions be in harmony with my
inner man. May I consider the wise man rich; and may I
have such wealth as only the self-restrained man can
endure.

PRAYER OF SOCRATES

❧

O thou Eternal One, may I commune
With thee, and for a moment bathe my soul
In thy infinity, Mother and Sire
Of all that are? In all that is art thou;
Being is but by thee, of thee, in thee;
Yet far thou reachest forth beyond the scope
Of space and time, or verge of human thought.
Transcendent God! Yet, ever immanent
In all that is, I flee to thee, and seek
Repose and soothing in my Mother's breast.
O God, I cannot fear, for thou art love,
And wheresoe'er I grope I feel thy breath!
Yea, in the storm which wrecks an argosy,
Or in the surges of the sea of men
When empires perish, I behold thy face,
I hear thy voice, which gives the law to all
The furies of the storm, and law proclaims,
"Peace, troubled waves, serve ye the right—be still!"

From all this dusty world thou wilt not lose
A molecule of earth nor spark of light.
I cannot fear a single flash of soul
Shall ever fail, outcast from thee, forgot.
Father and Mother of all things that are,
I flee to thee, and in thy arms find rest.
My God! how shall I thank thee for thy love?
Tears must defile my sacramental words,
And daily prayer be daily penitence
For actions, feelings, thoughts, which are amiss:
Yet will I not say, "God forgive!" for thou
Hast made the effect to follow cause, and bless
The erring, sinning man. Then let my sin
Continual find me out, and make me clean
From all transgression, purified and blest.

THEODORE PARKER

Praise be to God, sovereign Lord, Author of the
universe, who raises the winds and orders the morning,
worshiped in religion and the Lord of the worlds. Praise
be to God for his forbearance, when he knows all. Praise
be to God for his pardon, though he is all-powerful.
Praise be to God for his long-suffering in displeasure,
though he is well able to do what he chooses.

Praise be to God, Lord of creation, Source of all
livelihood, who orders the morning, Lord of majesty and
honor, of grace and beneficence, he who is so far that he
may not be seen and so near that he witnesses the secret
things. Blessed be he and forever exalted.

Praise be to God: he has no competitor to equal him
and no peer to compare with him, and no helper to aid
him. With his might he subdues the mighty and by his

greatness the great are humbled. Whatever he wills by his power he attains.

Praise be to God who hearkens to me when I call upon him, covers my unworthiness when I have been rebellious, and magnifies his grace upon me. I will not more transgress. I will sing to his praise and make mention of him in thanksgiving.

RAMADAN PRAYERS

These are thy glorious works, Parent of Good,
Almighty, thine this universal frame,
Thus wondrous fair; thyself how wondrous then!
Unspeakable, who sit'st above these heavens
To us invisible, or dimly seen
In these thy lowest works; yet these declare
Thy goodness beyond thought, and power divine.
Speak ye who best can tell, ye sons of light,
Angels; for ye behold him, and with songs
And choral symphonies, day without night,
Circle his throne rejoicing! ye in Heaven;
On earth join all ye creatures to extol
Him first, him last, him midst and without end.
Fairest of stars, last in the train of night,
If better thou belong not to the dawn,
Sure pledge of day, that crown'st the smiling morn
With thy bright circlet, praise him in thy sphere,
While day arises, that sweet hour of prime,
Thou Sun, of this great world both eye and soul,
Acknowledge him thy greater; sound his praise
In thy eternal course, both when thou climb'st,
And when high noon hast gained, and when thou
    fall'st.

Moon, that now meet'st the orient Sun, now fly'st,
With the fix'd stars, fix'd in their orb that flies,
And ye five other wand'ring fires that move
In mystic dance not without song, resound
His praise, who out of darkness called up light.
Air, and ye Elements, the eldest birth
Of Nature's womb, that in quaternion run
Perpetual circle, multiform, and mix
And nourish all things; let your ceaseless change
Vary to our great Maker still new praise.
Ye Mists and Exhalations that now rise
From hill or steaming lake, dusky or gray,
Till the Sun paint your fleecy skirts with gold,
In honor to the world's great Author rise,
Whether to deck with clouds the uncolored sky,
Or wet the thirsty earth with falling showers,
Rising or falling still advance his praise.
His praise, ye Winds, that from four quarters blow
Breathe soft or loud; and wave your tops, ye Pines,
With every plant; in sign of worship wave.
Fountains, and ye that warble, as ye flow,
Melodious murmurs, warbling, tune his Praise.
Join voices all ye living Souls; ye Birds,
That singing up to Heaven-gate ascend,
Bear on your wings and in your notes his praise.
Ye that in waters glide, and ye that walk
The earth, and stately tread, or lowly creep,
Witness if I be silent, morn or even,
To hill or valley, fountain or fresh shade,
Made vocal by my song, and taught his praise.
Hail, Universal Lord, be bounteous still
To give us only good; and if the night
Have gathered ought of evil, or concealed
Disperse it, as now light dispels the dark.

JOHN MILTON

❧

Grant us, we beseech thee, almighty and most merciful
God, fervently to desire, wisely to search out, and
perfectly to fulfill, all that is well pleasing unto thee.
Order thou our worldly condition to the glory of thy
name; and of all that thou requirest us to do grant us the
knowledge, the desire, and the ability, that we may fulfill
it as we ought; and that our path to thee may be safe,
straightforward, and perfect to the end.

SAINT THOMAS AQUINAS

❧

O most high, almighty, good Lord God, to thee belong
praise, glory, honor, and all blessing!
    Praised be my Lord God for all his creatures, and
especially for our brother the sun, who brings us the day
and who brings us the light; fair is he and shines with a
very great splendor: O Lord, he signifies to us thee!
    Praised be my Lord for our sister the moon, and for
the stars, the which he has set clear and lovely in heaven.
    Praised be my Lord for our brother the wind, and
for air and cloud, calms and all weather, by the which
thou upholdest life in all creatures.
    Praised be my Lord for our sister water, who is
very serviceable unto us and humble and precious and
clean.
    Praised be my Lord for our brother fire, through
whom thou givest us light in the darkness; and he is
bright and pleasant and very mighty and strong.
    Praised be my Lord for our mother the earth, the
which doth sustain us and keep us and bringeth forth
divers fruits and flowers of many colors, and grass.
    Praised be my Lord for all those who pardon one

another for his love's sake, and who endure weakness and tribulation: blessed are they who peaceably shall endure, for thou, O most highest, shalt give them a crown.

Praised be my Lord for our sister the death of the body, from which no man escapeth. Woe to him who dieth in mortal sin! Blessed are they who are found walking by thy most holy will, for the second death shall have no power to do them harm.

Praise ye and bless the Lord, and give thanks unto him, and serve him with great humility.

SAINT FRANCIS OF ASSISI

🌿

How poor is the wisdom of men, and how uncertain their forecast! Govern all by thy wisdom, O Lord, so that my soul may always be serving thee, as thou dost will and not as I may choose. Punish me not by granting that which I wish or ask, if it offend thy love, which would always live in me. Let me die to myself, that so I may serve thee: let me live to thee, thou who in thyself art the true life. Reign thou, and let me be the captive, for my soul covets no other freedom.

SAINT THERESA OF AVILA

12

....

Let the Redeemed
of the Lord Say So

Bach's 140th Cantata is called "Wachet auf" or "Sleepers Awake." When most people have an awakening it lies somewhere between "Eureka" and a gradual awareness of looking and seeing things differently. Having awakened, our desire is to share the experience, knowing that it can only be shared effectively with those willing to work on changing their own lives.

"Where your treasure is there will your heart be also," Jesus said. If our principles and values are small, then our attitudes, actions, and behaviors will also be small. On the other hand, if our values are rooted in principles of acceptance, courage, and wisdom, then the promise of a more abundant life is fulfilled.

The prophet Micah exhorts and encourages us: "Do justice, love mercy, and walk humbly with thy God."

We continue . . .

O give thanks to the Lord, for he is good; for his steadfast love endures forever! Let the redeemed of the Lord say so, whom he has redeemed from trouble and gathered in from the lands, from the east and from the west, from the north and from the south. Some wandered in desert wastes, finding no way to a city to dwell in; hungry and thirsty, their soul fainted within them. Then they cried to the Lord in their trouble, and he delivered them from their distress; he led them by a straight way, till they reached a city to dwell in. Let them thank the Lord for his steadfast love, for his wonderful works to the sons of men! For he satisfies him who is thirsty, and the hungry he fills with good things. Some sat in darkness and in gloom, prisoners in affliction and in irons, for they had rebelled against the words of God, and spurned the counsel of the Most High. Their hearts were bowed down with hard labor; they fell down, with none to help. Then they cried to the Lord in their trouble, and he delivered them from their distress; he brought them out of darkness and gloom, and broke their bonds asunder. Let them thank the Lord for his steadfast love, for his wonderful works to the sons of men! For he shatters the doors of bronze, and cuts in two the bars of iron. Some were sick through their sinful ways, and because of their iniquities suffered affliction; they loathed any kind of food, and they drew near to the gates of death. Then they cried to the Lord in their

trouble, and he delivered them from their distress; he
sent forth his word, and healed them, and delivered them
from destruction. Let them thank the Lord for his
steadfast love, for his wonderful works to the sons of
men! And let them offer sacrifices of thanksgiving, and
tell of his deeds in songs of joy! Some went down to the
sea in ships, doing business on the great waters; they saw
the deeds of the Lord, his wondrous works in the deep.
For he commanded, and raised the stormy wind, which
lifted up the waves of the sea. They mounted up to
Heaven, they went down to the depths; their courage
melted away in their evil plight; they reeled and
staggered like drunken men, and were at their wits' end.
Then they cried to the Lord in their trouble, and he
delivered them from their distress; he made the storm be
still, and the waves of the sea were hushed. Then they
were glad because they had quiet, and he brought them
to their desired haven. Let them thank the Lord for his
steadfast love, for his wonderful works to the sons of
men! Let them extol him in the congregation of the
people, and praise him in the assembly of the elders. He
turns rivers into a desert, springs of water into thirsty
ground, a fruitful land into a salty waste, because of the
wickedness of its inhabitants. He turns a desert into
pools of water, a parched land into springs of water. And
there he lets the hungry dwell, and they establish a city
to live in; they sow fields, and plant vineyards, and get a
fruitful yield. By his blessing they multiply greatly; and
he does not let their cattle decrease. When they are
diminished and brought low through oppression, trouble,
and sorrow, he pours contempt upon princes and makes
them wander in trackless wastes; but he raises up the
needy out of affliction, and makes their families like
flocks. The upright see it and are glad; and all

wickedness stops its mouth. Whoever is wise, let him give heed to these things; let men consider the steadfast love of the Lord.

PSALM 107

Fountain of life, perfection, and happiness, we lift our hearts to thee, the greatest, wisest, and best of beings. Give us, we pray thee, more worthy conceptions of thy nature and providence, better knowledge of thy truth and will; and, by fuller acquaintance with thee, may our souls find peace. Teach us to know ourselves. May we keep our hearts with all diligence, for out of them are the issues of life. In prosperity may we be humble, and in adversity patient. Save us from anger and malice. Give us prudence and constancy. And may we hold fast our integrity as long as we live. In every station may we discharge our duty, and find entrance to thy glorious kingdom.

UNITARIAN PRAYER

Life of my life, I shall ever try to keep my body pure, knowing that thy living touch is upon all my limbs.

I shall ever try to keep all untruths out from my thoughts, knowing that thou art that truth which has kindled the light of reason in my mind.

I shall ever try to drive all evils away from my heart and keep my love in flower, knowing that thou hast thy seat in the inmost shrine of my heart.

And it shall be my endeavor to reveal thee in my actions, knowing it is thy power gives me strength to act.

RABINDRANATH TAGORE

133

Boldly make a desperate push, man, as the saying is, for
prosperity, for freedom, for magnanimity. Lift up your
head, at last, as free from slavery. Dare to look up to
God, and say, Make use of me for the future as thou
wilt. I am of the same mind: I am equal with thee. I
refuse nothing which seems good to thee. Lead me
whither thou wilt. Clothe me in whatever dress thou
wilt. Is it thy will that I should be in a public or private
condition; dwell here, or be banished; be poor, or rich?
Under all these circumstances I will make thy defense to
men. I will show what the nature of everything is.

EPICTETUS.

The soul of him, who is self-conquered and full of peace,
is fixed on the Supreme, in cold and heat, in pleasure
and pain, in honor and dishonor. . . .

With soul at peace, with fear gone, standing firm in
the vow of service of the Eternal, controlling the mind,
with heart set on me, let him dwell in union, intent on
me. . . .

The seeker for union, thus ever joining himself in
union, his darkness gone, happily attains the infinite joy
of union with the Eternal.

He sees his soul as one with all beings, and all
beings as one with his soul; his soul joined in union,
beholding Oneness everywhere.

Who sees me everywhere, and sees all in me, him I
lose not, nor will he lose me. . . .

They who strive for freedom from age and death,
taking refuge in me, know the Eternal, the All, the
highest self, the perfect Work.

They who know me as the highest Being, the highest Divinity, the highest Sacrifice, even in death perceive me, their hearts united to me. . . .

I am the offering, I am the sacrifice, I am the oblation, I am the libation; I am the chant, I am the holy oil, I am the fire, I am what is offered.

I am the father of this world, the mother, the guardian, the father's father; I am the end of knowledge, the purifier, the sacred syllable, the hymn, the chant, the sacred sentence.

I am the way, the supporter, the lord, the witness, the home, the refuge, the beloved; the forthcoming and withdrawing, the place, the treasure, the everlasting seed.

I am equal toward all beings; nor is any hated or favored of me; but they who love me with dear love, they are in me and I in them.

BHAGAVAD-GITA

Those who develop respect and devotion
On hearing this supreme dedication,
Seeking supreme enlightenment,
Will be most blessed.

They will have abandoned all evils
And all bad associates
And will quickly see Infinite Light,
If they have this vow of enlightening practice.

Great is their gain, worthwhile their life,
Auspicious their birth as humans;
They will soon be like
The universally good enlightening being.

Those who have committed hellish crimes
Under the sway of ignorance
Will quickly put an end to them all
When this practice of good is expounded.

Endowed with knowledge, distinction, and
    nobility,
Invulnerable to false teachers and demons,
They will be honored
By all in the triple world.

They will quickly go to the
Tree of enlightenment
And sit there for the benefit
Of all living beings;
They will realize enlightenment,
Turn the wheel of teaching,
And conquer the devil
And all its cohorts.

Buddha knows those who hold this vow to
    practice good,
Who cause it to be told of and taught;
The fruit of this is supreme enlightenment—
Do not entertain any doubt.

As the hero Manjushri knows, so too does
    Universal Good;
As I learn from them I dedicate all this virtue.
By the supreme dedication praised by the buddhas
    of all times
I dedicate all this virtue to the practice of highest
    good.

Acting in accord with the time, may I
remove all obstructions,
May I see Infinite Light face to face and go to the
land of bliss.
There, may all these vows be complete;
Having fulfilled them, I will work for the weal of
all beings in the world.

Let me abide in the circle of that buddha,
born in a beautiful lotus,
And receive the prophecy of buddhahood there in
the presence
Of the buddha of Infinite Light.

Having received the prophecy there, with
millions of emanations
I will work for the weal of beings everywhere, by
the power of Buddha.

By whatever virtue I accumulate, having
invoked the vow to practice good,
May the pure aspiration of the world be at once all
fulfilled.

By the endless surpassing blessing realized
from dedication
To the practice of good,
May worldlings submerged in the torrent of passion
Go to the higher realm of Infinite Light.

BUDDHIST PRAYER

May the strength of God pilot us. May the power of God preserve us. May the wisdom of God instruct us. May the hand of God protect us. May the way of God direct us. May the shield of God defend us.

May the host of God guard us against the snares of the Evil One and the temptations of the world.

SAINT PATRICK

Grant to us, O Lord, to know that which is worth knowing, to love that which is worth loving, to praise that which pleaseth thee most, to esteem that which is most precious unto thee, and to dislike whatsoever is evil in thine eyes. Grant us with true judgment to distinguish things that differ, and above all to search out, and to do what is well pleasing unto thee, through Jesus Christ our Lord.

THOMAS À KEMPIS

Have mercy upon us.
Have mercy upon our efforts, that we
Before thee, in love and in faith,
Righteousness and humility,
May follow thee, with self-denial,
Steadfastness and courage,
And meet thee in the silence.

Give us a pure heart that we may see thee,
A humble heart that we may hear thee,
A heart of love that we may serve thee,
A heart of faith that we may live thee.

DAG HAMMARSKJÖLD

Thou madest us for thyself, and our heart is restless until
it find rest in thee.

Not with doubting but with assured consciousness
do I love thee, O Lord. Thou hast stricken my heart
with thy word and I loved thee. And the heavens, too,
and the earth and all that therein is, behold, on every
side they bid me love thee, nor cease to say so unto all.

But what do I love when I love thee? Not grace of
bodies nor the fair harmony of time, nor the brightness
of the light, so gladsome to our eyes; nor sweet melodies
of varied songs, nor the fragrant smell of flowers, of
ointments and spices, not manna and honey. None of
these love I when I love my God; and yet I love a kind
of light, and melody, and fragrance, a food, when I love
my God, the light, melody, fragrance, food of my inner
man: where there shineth unto my soul what space
cannot contain, and there soundeth what time beareth
not away, and there smelleth what breath disperseth not,
and there tasteth what eating diminisheth not, and there
clingeth what satiety divorceth not. This is what I love
when I love my God.

And what is this? I asked the earth and it answered
me, "I am not he." And whatsoever is in it confessed the
same. I asked the sea and the deeps, and the living
creeping things, and they answered, "We are not thy

God; seek above us." I asked the moving air; and the whole air with his inhabitants spoke, "Anaximenes was deceived; I am not God." I asked the heavens, sun, moon, stars. "Nor," say they, "are we the God whom thou seekest." And I replied unto all the things that encompass the door of my flesh: "Ye have told me of my God, that ye are not he; tell me something of him." And they cried out with a loud voice, "He made us." What then do I love when I love my God? By my soul will I ascend to him. See, I am mounting up through my mind toward thee. I will pass beyond this power of mind which is called memory, desirous to arrive at thee, and to cleave unto thee.

How then do I seek thee, O Lord? For when I seek thee, I seek a happy life. I will seek thee that my soul may live. For my body liveth by my soul, and my soul by thee. Nor is it I alone nor some few besides, but we all would fain be happy. Happy then will my soul be when, no distraction interposing, it shall joy in that only Truth, by whom all things are true.

Too late I loved thee, O thou Beauty of Ancient Days, yet ever new! Behold, thou wert within—and I abroad, and there I searched for thee. Thou wert with me, but I was not with thee. When I shall with my whole self cleave to thee, I shall nowhere have sorrow or labor, and my life shall wholly live as wholly full of thee.

SAINT AUGUSTINE

Let nothing disturb thee,
Let nothing affright thee.
All things are passing.
God never changes.

Patience gains all things.
Who has God wants nothing.
God alone suffices.

SAINT THERESA OF AVILA

ㅎ

God, grant me the serenity to accept the things I cannot change, courage to change the things I can, and wisdom to know the difference.

REINHOLD NIEBUHR